ON BECOMING A TEACHER

ON BECOMING
A TEACHER

Herbert Kohl

METHUEN | LONDON

First published in 1984 by Harper & Row
in the USA under the title *Growing Minds*.

First published in Great Britain in 1986 by
Methuen & Co. Ltd
11 New Fetter Lane, London EC4P 4EE

Printed in Great Britain by St Edmundsbury Press,
Bury St Edmunds, Suffolk

British Library Cataloguing in Publication Data

Kohl, Herbert R.
On becoming a teacher.
1. Teaching
I. Title
371.1'02   LB1025.2

ISBN 0-416-42010-9

CONTENTS

ACKNOWLEDGEMENTS

Grateful acknowledgement is made for permission to reprint:

Lines from 'September, 1, 1939', W. H. Auden, *The English Auden: Poems, Essays and Dramatic Writings, 1927–1939*, ed. Edward Mendelson. 'September, 1, 1939' copyright 1940, renewed 1968 by W. H. Auden. Reprinted by permission of Random House, Inc.

Lines from 'Another Brick in the Wall', Roger Waters, copyright © 1979 by Pink Floyd Music Publishers Ltd. All rights reserved. Used by permission of Unichappell Music, Inc. and Pink Floyd Music Publishers Ltd.

'A Letter to Jose', Victor Hernandez Cruz. Reprinted by permission of the author.

FOREWORD

Herbert Kohl is a teacher and a writer. He has written at least one book about teaching that deserves to become a classic, *36 Children*, one very popular guide for teachers, *The Open Classroom*, some fine children's books, and a host of useful theoretical and practical works on teaching and living. This book describes what it is like to grow into the craft or profession of teaching, and the idea behind it strikes me as an excellent one. One of the troubles about America today is that we don't know enough—about institutions, about how lives get lived over time, about how people learn to make their living and what they do all day. People feel funny telling you how they spend the working day, as though they might bore you with shoptalk. And yet other people's work is one of the great topics of conversation, like sex or religion or politics. Unless we begin to hear each other's stories, we'll keep walking around like strangers in an airport. And we will certainly not provide the young with the guidance they need to end up doing something worthwhile that suits them.

At any rate, here it is: part memoir, part manifesto for a certain stance toward teaching and young people, part vade mecum for an apprentice teacher or someone thinking about teaching. An attractive, characteristically informal book—

above all an encounter with a fierce, loving classroom character with flyaway hair and a glint in his eye, a demonic trickster intent on getting you to learn set theory or *Macbeth* or why the flounder has an eye that migrates from one side of its head to the other.

Kohl's family was in the construction business. He claims never to have left it. Teaching is learning how people construct selves and helping them to do the job better. Although there are no unmixed motives, Kohl argues that most teachers embark on the life out of altruism, the desire to share what they love, and to empower other people. Teachers are pilgrims of a certain kind of quest. Growth fascinates them: they are called to spend a lifetime encountering the mystery and excitement of development.

Kohl tells stories about some of the exemplary early teachers he's had, who lived for their subjects and taught him to love poetry and music. He has a fine sketch of a Harvard math teacher, too, a tribute to a kind of open-ended and profoundly intellectual teaching that is rare at any level.

He had fantasies of being a teacher when he was little. He flopped trying to teach his brothers checkers, but he learned a lot tutoring a boy with cerebral palsy. Kohl graduated from Harvard, where few people expect to become schoolteachers, much less elementary school ones. He did graduate work at Oxford and Columbia in philosophy, but then the urge to teach overtook him, and he took a job in a school for disturbed kids in New York.

He got his first public school assignment in 1962. Already he had worked out an idea of the kind of classroom he wanted to run: it was to be a place full of materials and different things to learn, where kids could make choices among intellectually exciting options, where the drama of themes and topics and big organizing questions was central to children's work, and where conversation itself was a key educational medium. The name for this style of teaching changes from decade to decade, but clearly Kohl had already lined himself up as a progressive who was working out what at different times would have been called the project method or informal or open education—the name hardly matters, since slogans are the curse of educational discussions. Kohl wonders if he might have gotten better training in his chosen mode of teaching if he had graduated from Teachers College in the progressive twenties or thirties. Still, the ideas were there, as they have been perennially since the nineteenth century: active learning on the children's part, lots of materials, themes, and conversation are the staples of a certain tradition of classroom teaching that is especially rich and well-worked-out with younger children. Froebel, Pestalozzi, Parker, Dewey, Montessori have all contributed a store of examples, materials, and ideas to this mode of practice, as Kohl has come to be aware. His historical sense of these issues—his knowledge that there is a history to build on—is rare among American teachers and is the fruit of his own teaching maturity. But as a young teacher in the early sixties, Kohl was as ignorant of the pedagogical past as any of the innovators of the late sixties, groping along, as Americans tend to do, in the United States of Amnesia.

Kohl chronicles the classic mistakes of a beginning teacher: he let the kids call him "Herb" instead of "Mr. Kohl," and then found himself mistrusted by other teachers and the principal. New teachers, young themselves, are often not clear whether they belong with the grownups or the kids. This uncertainty bedevils their practice. Like others before and after him, Kohl struggled to know when and how to get on and off his high horse. He faced up to classroom bullies. He persisted, and some fine things started to happen: there's a lovely account of what happened to the class when some kids started drawing blueprints of their apartments. Kohl was evolving into the artful teacher of *36 Children*.

Kohl talks about that elusive subject the craft of teaching in more general terms too. Teaching is like acting or conducting, or being a musician: not easy to put into words. Kohl pushes on the words, trying to use examples to pin the butterfly down. A study of a friend's teaching offers him an instance of what he means by "sensibility." And telling stories, he tries to show that good teachers love students as learners—that love is a significant part of the teacher's commitment, though this can't mean loving every unpleasant or unlovable student. The love he means is abstract, like a love of justice, but it is tied in a teacher's case to confronting the specific student who doesn't understand or can't sit still. Kohl talks about the need to lose your own ego as a teacher, and gives cases of the teacher as a detached student of the human beings he or she teaches. He describes the teacher as trickster in his work with Alice, a teenager in a prison school. He discusses problem kids and discipline, and the way that a good teacher has to become, willy-nilly, something of an expert at life in groups, rightly insisting that a key part of good teaching is making it possible for even unhappy kids to feel welcome in a group.

As a practitioner, Kohl speaks for a progressive tradition that emphasizes a rich blend of intellectual content, active learning, conversation, and what might be called serious play. This tradition is sometimes caricatured by both its friends and its critics. A standard criticism of progressive education since the nineteenth century has been its neglect of content. Kohl, with his commitment to teaching kids to think, is profoundly critical of the mindlessness of some child-centered education. Teaching, he says, is not just getting kids to feel good, but to understand, to know, to have skills, above all to think. The interaction of children's minds and feelings with the curriculum is the true locus of good teaching and good learning; any approach that stresses the child at the expense of content, or the curriculum at the expense of the child, is simply unsound.

This fundamental point—that the problem of teaching is the interaction of child and content, not emphasizing one over the other—needs to be made now more than ever. The American educational system has plenty of examples of get-the-kids-feeling-good and many more examples of deadening mechanical applications of textbooks, workbooks, and other overpackaged materials. Both are anti-intellectual in their separate ways. What is rare is to find classrooms where teachers are encouraged to create a living connection between children's minds and the material.

The problems with this kind of teaching are, of course, its demands. If your material is going to be like a branching tree, along which children can travel in different ways and which the teacher can take advantage of in the course of the group's evolution, then clearly the teacher has to be soaked in the material. You need lots of ideas, lots of stuff, and a great curiosity about what you're teaching. Kohl gives examples—a unit on sound, for instance, that led to interesting work. But I'd like to have read more on the subject of the curriculum. He mentions problems—how much teachers need to know, for example. He does point out that good teachers in this mode build up a repertoire of favorite topics and themes and materials over the years, rather like a musician tackling Mozart or an actor working up aspects of Shakespeare, and the long-term perspective should be a help. But we need more specific advice to offer working teachers or eager new apprentices. It seems an enormous pity that there have been so few ways to chronicle and catalogue the inventive classroom work of the last twenty years; it got buried, just as the best work of the progressive era did. In the United States of Amnesia, we keep having to reinvent everything from scratch, and this is one reason why educational practice doesn't develop in a cumulative way.

Kohl may be skimpy on the subject of curriculum, but he is dead right that our age of packaging is generally indifferent to the contents of the package. Here, embodied in twenty years of practice, is the right idea, the point: In teaching, what we ought to be aiming at is what he calls a certain kind of intellectual sophistication. Intellectual sophistication is a matter of how students learn to use their minds; how they employ abstract thinking, multiple lines of thought; whether they can see ideas as whole systems and reason about them systematically. A gentler if more formidable way to put this is to say that Kohl is making a plea for classrooms in which teachers and students can take time for what the Germans call *Sprache* —serious, continuing discussion, thoughtful speech.

It would be an immense gain if our growing national conversation on education could encourage teachers to conceive of the job as creating settings for intelligent discussion. Thoughtful speech, informed dialogue, the mutual exploration of ideas and materials—these manifestations of *Sprache* ought to be the ideal, yet in fact occasions and settings for good talk are as rare in the schools as they are in the rest of a society under the spell of "we talk, you listen."

Conversation and discussion are the real paths to thinking. Kohl's two major criticisms of our schools blend: they are not, on the whole, good environments for growth and individuality, and they are not, on the whole, settings in which students learn to think more clearly.

Kohl is somewhat scornful of the national obsession with test scores, as I am, yet the most sensible interpretation of current test results is that although younger children may be taught to decode better than they used to be, they are not encouraged to use their minds and to think. The passivity of students in the later years is a tremendous problem.

His convictions about content led him to reshape his own practice. He has done excellent work, for example, in the area of writing, but he is now moving from pure improvisation to work that builds more on classical and historical foundations—work that has more content, in other words. Most student improvisation in writing derives from personal experience, TV, the movies, and popular novels—which are, as he says, often a rather shallow base. He is dismayed by the language and thought students pick up from the media. Why should their world be limited to this thin and stupid stuff? Why not have them read Shakespeare, Aristophanes, Rabelais?

At his summer camp for seven-to-fourteen-year-olds, Kohl now does plays. Each summer the group puts on a production of an edited version of *A Midsummer Night's Dream, Antigone, Tartuffe,* or, most recently, *Macbeth.* The drama is done in the spirit of teaching intellectual sophistication and serious play. Kohl's account of the *Macbeth* production is a fine example of progressive practice that values thought and content.

As a guide to new teachers, this book is valuable for its particularly levelheaded, concrete theory and its clear sense of the challenge of teaching: the mysteriousness, the drama, and the excitement. Teaching, Kohl says, is "like wanting to have children or to write or paint or dance or invent or think through a mathematical problem that only a few have been able to solve." No one could doubt after reading this little book that teaching is an imaginative feat—an art, in fact—and the flavor of Kohl's own mastery and artistry is unmistakable.

New teachers would probably benefit the most from the passages where Kohl is thinking through the tensions of the job, as when he took over a K-1 classroom in Berkeley:

> There are twenty-nine strangers to meet and get to know and understand. There is subject matter to structure and present. There is time to fill up. There are details to deal with—late and absence notes, attendance forms, missing lunches, lost coats, sweaters, and hats. . . . Should you concentrate on discovering who the students are and how their energy can be focused and lean on workbooks and mechanical exercises for a while, or would it be better to concentrate on interesting content, well presented, and be a strict disciplinarian until you and your students get to know each other better? I've never been able to decide which strategy to use, and I go back and forth for a few

months until feeling and content come together. In a new teaching situation, I do, however, always begin in a more structured way than I will come to. It is easier to loosen up than to tighten up. Relaxing rules and structures is seen as an act of trust and affection, tightening up as a punishment if not a covert declaration of war.

In fact, new and experienced teachers would welcome more discussion of the troubles and problems of the craft than they will find here. Kohl is by temperament an activist and optimist; what sticks in his reader's mind are his victories. This is an upbeat book at a very downbeat time for education nationally. That's all right, but it would be a further help if experienced teachers like Kohl would begin to write of the despair of teaching too. What about the panicky feeling veteran teachers get when they wonder what the point is? What about the feeling of running dry?

This is not to say that Kohl plays a relentlessly glad game. He says: "I am sorry to make learning to teach well seem like such a lonely activity, but it has been that way for me." What help can teachers get for this intolerable loneliness? Kohl doesn't say. He asks, without really answering, how teachers will encounter a more demanding vision of teaching if it is not in the curriculum, not part of teacher training, and not discussed by colleagues.

The educational reforms of the sixties and seventies (in which Kohl himself was a central figure) were a profoundly mixed bag, but at least the reform climate alerted working teachers to the possibility of alternatives to the way they were teaching; they learned of other kindred spirits; they often got support for reworking classroom practice. Now, in teaching, as in other parts of society, alternatives are scarce as hen's teeth, and for the moment, at least, hope is at a low ebb.

Kohl wonders whether he would have become a teacher now, in the eighties, when jobs are hard to find, the public schools are under attack, and teaching is in disrepute as a profession. Certainly in the sixties there was more public honor for those who tried to help others than there is in President Reagan's narcissistic America. Teaching, the civil rights movement, and the idea of public service were respected; and there was more optimism about public education than there is right now.

However, Kohl answers, the children are still there; they are the main reason to become a teacher. Perhaps the time to redouble our efforts to care for children and educate them is a time of public neglect and indifference like the present. If not now, when? If not us, who?

Kohl is not at present working in a public school. He runs his summer camp, and his various projects keep him in touch with kids and public school classrooms and colleagues, but he has taken a different path. Others of his friends have chosen to stay on in the public schools and fight the battle at an unpropitious time.

Still, Kohl is speaking for those thousands who have stayed on in the struggle one way or another, for all the long-distance runners who started out the race young and radical and full of new energy and who now run on their second or third wind, determined to stay in the race for the long haul. Anyone reading this book can begin to savor what it means to stick to a craft over time, to be seasoned and shaped by it. Kohl is not yet an old pro, but he is a veteran who knows his work well and loves it and will continue at it over the years, gathering wisdom and getting better at it as he goes. There are in fact many people like him in our society, but to say they are not generally honored for being in for the long haul is putting it mildly. A narcissistic society worships youth but hates the young, because it envies them and fears growing old; it hates the old, too, and generally does not honor cumulative experience. Today's young, facing the throwaway society, need to meet people like Kohl, to see what it means to have found a lifelong calling.

This business of time is so important, as the poets keep telling us. We all have lessons to learn. In a memorable passage in *36 Children* one of Kohl's Harlem students tells him, "Mr. Kohl, one good year is not enough." As a young teacher, Kohl accepted that, and felt defeated, despite all his wonderful work. Now, as we get older, my guess is that Kohl and many of the rest of us are getting a sharper picture of both the limits on what a lone teacher can do, and of how important a year is in someone's life. One good year can be a very great deal, after all. This is the sort of truth that comes easier to the middle-aged, after twenty years' experience, than to the young; that is another lesson this valuable book can teach us.

—JOSEPH FEATHERSTONE

PART I

BEGINNING TO TEACH

Growing Minds is factually accurate, except that names and individual traits have been changed where necessary.

1.

GROWTH

Ever since I was a child, the details of growth have fascinated me. I remember wondering how babies learned to walk and talk, how grownups learned to dance, read, and drive cars and trucks, but mostly about how buildings grew on empty lots. My father, grandfather, and uncles were all in the construction business and often they took me to their jobs and let me wander around. I saw structures rise, saw the guts of buildings assembled and then concealed. My relatives always had many jobs going simultaneously, each in a different state of development. On one the site was being cleared, on another the basic structure was being created. Some jobs were almost done and plasterers, lathe workers, and cabinetmakers were putting in the details and painters finishing the surfaces.

In time, the work my relatives did became a central metaphor for my perception of growth in people. I didn't want to work with bricks and steel and wood, but with children. Yet as a teacher I've always thought of myself as part of the construction business. All of us are in different stages of completion or renovation, and none of us is ever without the need for some kind of building. A teacher has to become a construction expert, someone who knows how to help draw together skills and resources to create a harmonious functioning whole, or who knows how to renovate a structure that is dysfunctional or damaged.

My father's expertise was renovation. One Sunday he and my grandfather took me to a job they were thinking of bidding on. The job was to put in stores on the first two floors of an old twenty-story apartment building and to convert the next five floors to offices. My grandfather had the blueprints of the building, which he read without effort even though he never learned to read English. I watched both of them carefully because they were doing things that seemed very strange to me. My grandfather would go to a certain place at the front of the building and bang a long nail through the brickwork. My father tapped on the wall in several places. Then they took a ladder out of the truck and climbed up the face of the building about a story and did the same things. I could feel that they were becoming very tense but couldn't figure out what was happening until my grandfather said, "Those son-of-a-bitches dropped half the beams. This thing shouldn't be standing up anymore."

My father explained to me that some builders eliminated a beam here, a girder there, to make more profit. He added that you could never trust plans to reveal the actual structure of a building. You had to probe the building itself, let it reveal itself. If you bid a job simply on the basis of the blueprints, you'd likely end up cheated and put your workers in danger.

In looking at young people growing, I've learned to apply the same ideas. A child is not an abstraction that can be fitted neatly into some scheme or theory, for growth never quite fits the laws of development psychologists invent. You have to discover who a child is by tapping and probing gently before a plan for construction or reconstruction can be developed. And you have to love to see a beautiful structure emerge, to have pride, as my father and grandfather did, in doing a good job.

Of course, people are not buildings and that's what makes

observing their growth so interesting. Buildings do not build themselves, but people do. Understanding the complex relationships between self-growth and nurturing growth is essential to becoming a good teacher. Further, the love of nurturing and observing growth in others is essential to sustaining a life of teaching. This implies that no matter what you teach or how you present yourself to your students, you have to be on the learners' side and to believe that they can and will grow during the time you are together. I am not sure of how that belief develops, yet it is characteristic of every fine teacher I've known.

During my first few years of teaching I tenaciously held to the belief that if only I tried hard enough, every one of my students would read, write, calculate and, even better, find some aspect of knowledge to master in depth. Some students, however, challenged that belief (or, more accurately, article of faith) to the extreme—indeed, the harder I tried to get them to learn, the more resistant they became. James Donald, for example, seemed to resent any implication that he was teachable. He was sixteen, two years older than any other student in my sixth-grade class and more than four years older than most of them. He spent the entire day sitting rigidly at his desk, fists and jaws clenched. He never looked at me, refused to respond to questions, refused to laugh at what other students found funny. He didn't play tricks and wasn't defiant. He just sat in his remoteness, driving me to try the craziest tactics to get him to try to read or write. Grades didn't mean anything to him, even praise didn't seem to touch him. He was doing his time, and despite my greatest efforts he didn't pick up a book or pencil or crack a smile throughout the whole year. The only thing he did with pleasure was play an aggressive, not graceful but extremely focused and effective game of basketball.

This happened during my third year of teaching. I didn't

have children of my own yet and still could give twelve hours a day to my students. Every day after school I ran a basketball league. James was one of the stars even though he didn't talk even on the court. He took on the biggest, toughest players and intimidated them all. He played smart basketball, anticipated other people's moves, passed so accurately he always had as many assists as points even though he was high scorer in most games. He was all intelligence on the court. Yet I couldn't do anything with him in the classroom. It would have been easy to quit on James, but I found myself reaching for new methods, techniques, ideas. Even though I found nothing that worked with him, I felt I was learning ways to reach other resistant, educationally damaged youngsters.

I met James about four years after he left my class. He had just finished his junior year at a high school in the Bronx and was all-city honorable mention in basketball. James was friendly for the first time since I'd known him, though his fists and jaws were no more relaxed than they were in the sixth grade. He told me he had loved to watch me try to teach him, that it was a battle of wills and he had been determined to win. But he also told me that he had listened even though he never responded to me and that he had taught himself to read and write well enough to stay in high school and play ball. He also thanked me for not throwing him out of the class.

Students like James have continued to confirm my perhaps irrational belief that all youngsters can learn despite any handicaps and that good teaching consists to a large degree in being obsessed with helping others grow.

2.

ALTRUISM:

THE CALLING TO TEACH

I believe the impulse to teach is fundamentally altruistic and represents a desire to share what you value and to empower others. Of course, all teachers are not altruistic. Some people teach in order to dominate others or to support work they'd rather do or simply to earn a living. But I am not talking about the job of teaching so much as the calling to teach. Most teachers I know, even the most demoralized ones, who drag themselves to oppressive and mean schools where their work is not respected and their presence not welcome, have felt that calling at some time in their lives.

Between the ages of ten and twelve, many children have running-away-from-home fantasies. This was certainly true for me and for my friends growing up in the Bronx in the late 1940s. Bobby dreamed of going down to the seamen's hall and shipping out to Hong Kong on a tramp steamer. Ronnie wanted to hitchhike to Chicago and become a boxer. Marilyn swore she would join the Haganah and be a freedom fighter in Israel. My fantasy was so bizarre that I was afraid to tell it to my friends. I wanted to run off to a small rural town in the Midwest and become an elementary school teacher.

No one in the family ever suggested I become a teacher and none of my relatives were teachers. I had two teachers, however, who were as sensitive to the growth of their students as my father and grandfather were to the quality of the structures they built, and who inspired me to want to teach. Mrs. Cooper was my kindergarten teacher. I don't remember anything about her class, but I do remember vividly meeting her on the street throughout my elementary and junior high school days and chatting with her about all my classmates and their brothers and sisters. She never forgot the name or face of any student she taught during her forty years at P.S. 82 and used to say she was more interested in how her former pupils grew after they left her than how well they did in her class. She was the repository of the neighborhood's memory and helped arrange class reunions, connect people with jobs, and provide information about marriages and births and deaths. She had only good to say about her former pupils. No matter how they turned out, they were still kindergarten children to her, beginning to learn their way in a difficult world. Considering the number of people who asked for her advice or who shared information with her, she seemed to me more active as a teacher after her retirement than even during her days in kindergarten.

Mrs. Cooper was respected by everybody in the neighborhood and welcome in every home. She was a model of kindness and generosity in the midst of a harsh, sometimes violent environment, and I remember wanting to command similar respect when I grew up. She made teaching seem like the most honored work one could do.

The other teacher who influenced me was Mrs. Lennon. She revealed to our fifth-grade class that the world was much larger than and different from the Bronx. Of course, we had all been told or read that the world had many peoples and cultures, and also that the arts were important. But Mrs. Lennon showed us. She described her travels and told us about the people she met and talked to. I think my romantic notion of the Midwest as a place of freedom and beauty came from her description of several small towns at the foothills of the Rockies where she had vacationed and made a number of friends.

Every day in class we listened to classical music and looked at classical or modern paintings. She read from novels to open the day and usually closed the day with a poem. I didn't understand or like most of what she presented to us, but I didn't resist it since I could see that she put her whole being into her presentations. She hummed with the music, would tell us to listen to the violins or trumpets, would repeat a line or two of poetry several times, almost singing it. And she told us not to bother trying to like or understand what she exposed us to, just to open ourselves up and listen and look. She explained that she was just planting seeds and that it would take time for them to grow in us. I had never known anyone so serious about art, literature, and music or so curious about the way people lived. Somehow these seeds she planted, some of which sprouted within me, as well as her obvious love of the thirty-nine eleven-year-olds she shared her experiences with, led me to believe that a teacher's life was exciting. You could travel and learn, you could start in the Bronx and maybe even become a teacher in the Midwest, showing what you know about New York and at the same time learning about the country and the mountains. You could help other people learn things about the world that they never imagined existed and share your enthusiasms.

Inspired by her, I decided to try teaching and recruited my younger brother and his friends as students. At eleven, my image of what teachers did was fairly simple. A teacher told students things they didn't know and showed them how to do things they couldn't do. In addition, a teacher had to make sure the students learned what they were told and that they didn't fool around too much.

I decided to teach Ted and four of his friends how to play checkers. I knew how to play checkers and they didn't; and I felt confident that I could control five seven-year-olds. Thus I met all my criteria for qualifying as a teacher and saw no reason why I shouldn't succeed.

My first and last session with Ted and his friends was a disaster. I set up the checkerboard and explained how the pieces are placed and how they move. Ted and Jay listened carefully and moved the pieces diagonally, just as I'd shown them. Jumping was next. Jay seemed to get the idea, but Ted jumped three spaces, jumped his own pieces, jumped from black to red, jumped everywhere but where he was supposed to. I was beginning to lose my patience when I noticed Tommy and Paul. They were supposed to be waiting patiently at the other board. Instead they were building towers out of checkers and throwing marbles at them. The checkers were all over the room. I don't know why it took me so long to discover that. By the time I got them to pick up the checkers and set their board up, Ted and Jay were building towers. I remember getting angry at my brother, calming down, and then getting really angry at him the next day when he told me that he and his friends had known how to play checkers all along and that they had decided to take lessons from me in order to annoy me by pretending not to learn. It was the first but certainly not the last time in my teaching career when the students were in control.

3.

AN UNEXPECTED
OPPORTUNITY

My first serious opportunity to teach came when I was a junior in high school. My chemistry teacher called me aside after class one day and offered me a job. He explained to me that his son had cerebral palsy and couldn't attend school. He offered me five dollars a week if I'd come to his home several afternoons after school and teach his son to read. I had no idea of how to teach reading, but I accepted the challenge anyway.

My first meeting with Roger was awkward. Though he was my age, his body was small and twisted. His hands seemed to be put on backward and he had to make an enormous effort to say a simple sentence. I couldn't help staring at him and feeling frightened and embarrassed in his presence. At the same time, I was angry at myself for such an unfeeling response. He pretended not to notice my awkwardness, and as we got to know each other better he told me that he expected people to treat him like a freak. He was no longer angry at that response, simply resigned to it.

Another thing that struck me that first day was the brightness of his eyes. It was as if the paralysis of his body forced him to direct all his energy up to his eyes in order to engage the world and communicate with people.

I brought a number of books with me, ranging from my sister's fourth-grade reader to my own school texts. I also had a copy of *The Collected Poetry of W. H. Auden*, which I always carried with me. Roger looked at Roz's books with scorn and informed me that he could read easy books. Then he pointed to the Auden book and asked me what it was. I explained that it was a collection of poems that moved me and that I loved to flip through the book and read it on the subway or in the small café downtown where I used to hang out on weekends.

He said he'd never read a poem. The only books he read were schoolbooks or simple storybooks. I picked a favorite poem and began to read:

> I sit in one of the dives
> On Fifty-second Street
> Uncertain and afraid
> As the clever hopes expire . . .

He interrupted: "What's a dive? What does Fifty-second Street look like?"

I tried to answer his questions and realized that his problem with reading had nothing to do with the mechanics of reading. It had to do with the limitation of experience imposed upon him by his handicap. He wasn't mobile and only knew the world from the perspective of his wheelchair and the radio. I described a dive, in fact a lot of dives on Fifty-second Street. I knew most of them and used to spend Saturdays sitting in one or another of them imagining I was in the same place Auden had written about and hoping he still spent time in dives on Fifty-second Street and I could meet him.

We went through Auden's poem line by line, talking about Nijinsky, Diaghilev, the Common Man, Eros, and other references in the poem. Fortunately I had a wonderful high school teacher who knew how to spend a week reading and analyzing a short poem with our class and make the poem fresh and alive at the end of the process. Most English teachers I've known analyzed things to death. Mrs. Berstein analyzed them to life. I used what I learned in her class to read Auden and pretended to be her when reading and talking about poetry with Roger.

I remember lingering over the last lines:

> May I, composed like them
> Of Eros and of dust,
> Beleaguered by the same
> Negations and despair
> Show an affirming flame.

The last line was particularly moving for Roger. He said he had always thought of being infirm and he saw from Auden how infirm everyone was and how affirmation was more important than indulging infirmity.

We shared many other poems. They dealt with issues that moved us—with war and censorship (this was during the McCarthy era, and many people we knew were victimized), with courage and unrequited love, and with longing for strengths neither of us had.

Roger took to poetry and literature. We spent several afternoons a week reading and talking together. On weekends he got his parents to drive him around Manhattan so he could see more of the world, and he also convinced them to take him to the theater and to movies. The inconvenience of moving him around was worth it as he began to figure out ways to become more independent and engaged in the world. I could witness his becoming more independent and felt good about being part of his new experience. He didn't seem to mind the extra effort he had to make to leave his apartment and become mobile. Watching him made me feel for perhaps the first time in my life that I'd done something that had a powerful and positive effect on the life of another person.

Roger and I became friends and the lessons continued

until I graduated from high school and left the Bronx to attend college. I always felt guilty about being paid to read with Roger, who taught me as much as I taught him and became more a friend than a student.

4.

THE PERSISTENCE
OF MY FANTASY

My fantasy about being an elementary school teacher maintained its strength throughout college, though I never told anybody about it until the week before my graduation from Harvard. My tutor asked me what I wanted to do after graduation and in a moment of intimacy I shared my dream with him. He laughed and expressed a viewpoint I was to hear many times after that: "People don't go to Harvard to become elementary school teachers."

After graduation I spent a year on a scholarship at Oxford and then returned to New York, where I studied philosophy at Columbia University. Elementary school teaching was still on my mind, but graduate school was comfortable and I put off making a decision about teaching until I passed my comprehensive exams for a Ph.D. in philosophy and was a year or two away from settling down as an assistant professor at some university. The thought of sitting in class and seminar room and talking about sense data and other philosophical esoterica for the rest of my life was grim. I wanted to be among children, to meet all kinds of people, to live in a world more like the Bronx than Harvard.

At the age of twenty-four I took the step I'd always wanted to take. I didn't go to that small town in the Midwest, but first to a school for severely disturbed children and then to a ghetto community in New York. Now, twenty-one years later, I live in a small rural town in northern California and still work with elementary and junior high school youngsters.

What was it that made teaching children more romantic to me than medicine, business, mathematics, or other careers I've flirted with? And why is it that teaching young children is as interesting and challenging now in Point Arena, California, as it was in Harlem and Berkeley and the other places in which I've taught? The only answer I find even partially satisfactory is that the romance of teaching is related less to individual students than to the phenomena of growth itself. It is wonderful to witness young people discovering that they can have power and to be able to help them acquire the skills and sensitivity they need to achieve the goals they come to set for themselves.

Wanting to teach is like wanting to have children or to write or paint or dance or invent or think through a mathematical problem that only a few have been able to solve. It has an element of mystery, involving as it does the yearly encounter with new people, the fear that you will be inadequate to meet their needs, as well as the rewards of seeing them become stronger because of your work. And as is true of the other creative challenges, the desire to teach and the ability to teach well are not the same thing. With the rarest of exceptions, one has to learn how to become a good teacher just as one has to learn how to become a scientist or an artist.

After withdrawing from graduate school at Columbia, I went to the New York City Board of Education to apply for a teacher's license. In 1960 there were hundreds of teaching jobs available in the city schools, and I assumed my education alone qualified me for one of them. The first secretary to the assistant superintendent in charge of licensing and credentials gave me several forms to fill out. She looked over my forms and told me to wait. An hour later, another secretary took the forms and told me she'd be right with me. After another hour, she returned and referred me to a third secretary, who handed me a sheet of paper informing me that I had no education courses and therefore didn't qualify for any teaching job in the system. I began to explain to her that I had taught math during summer school at Harvard, had experience working with youngsters, knew a lot about literature and science. She paid no attention and simply referred me back to the first secretary, who told me that the best thing was to enroll at Teachers College, Columbia, or at the ed school at NYU. I pleaded to talk to someone higher up and was politely informed that everyone was busy and that there was nothing for me to talk about anyway, that qualifications were qualifications. Trying to get someone to listen to you at 110 Livingston Street was like trying to kick down the Empire State Building.

There was no way I would return to college at that point in my life. A friend of mind told me that private schools didn't have the same requirements as public schools, and so I got a private school directory and went from school to school asking if a job was available. I began alphabetically and got down to the *L*'s before hearing of a teaching job that was open and didn't require a credential. I heard of it through the League School, which served severely disturbed children. The secretary there, who was the opposite of the public school gatekeepers I'd encountered, told me of an opening at the Reece School for the Severely Disturbed. I went immediately and was hired after a half-hour interview with Mrs. Reece. It was Thursday and I was to begin on Monday. I asked if there was any preparation to make. Mrs. Reece assured me that I'd learn on the job.

5.

MY FIRST JOB

I was a teacher at last. Even though the salary was three hundred dollars a month and I didn't have the slightest idea of what or how well I'd do with my students, I remember walking, practically skipping, down Lexington Avenue from Ninety-fourth Street, where the school was, to my apartment on Eighty-fourth, feeling giddy with excitement. Being paid to teach—doing what I'd dreamed of doing and being paid too—how wonderful could the world be?

Elation gave way to anxiety Sunday night, and by Monday morning I had visions of being rejected by a class of twenty-five bizarre children. What was a severely disturbed child and what did he or she do in school? What could be done for them? Did they grow like normal children? Would my job merely be custodial or would there be excitement to it? I walked slowly up Lexington Avenue to school Monday morning wondering if I really wanted to teach that much.

The school was located in a three-story brownstone and the classroom I was assigned to work in was on the top floor. I was introduced to Sarah, the other third-floor teacher, who was my supervisor. The class we were to share was unlike anything I'd ever experienced during my own schooling. There were only five ten- and eleven-year-old boys in the class and I was expected to work with only two of them and help out with a third. Sarah had an organization chart that showed me how every minute of the day was to be spent and gave me copies of the workbooks my students were using at the moment. From that first day throughout my stay at the Reece School I was a "by-the-book" teacher and followed the school's routine and its curriculum. It was a secure if not particularly creative way for me to begin my career, especially as my students' behavior required constant monitoring and they needed regular, predictable tasks to perform.

John and Fred were the boys assigned to me, and Harry, the most remote and the saddest child in the class, was with me part time. Sarah worked with him the rest of the day, as well as with Roger and the several Tommy Rinaldos we had to contend with. Tommy was a concentrated energy force who lived many lives on many planets, and his condition often determined how our day went. There were times when he was charming and other times when he became so wild and obsessed with images and phantoms that he had to be held down. He might become the Tommy Rinaldo Broadcasting Company and predict doom for the world as he tore through the school destroying everything in sight and crying at the same time. Or he would hold conversations with the generals in his imaginary army, Sisbeer and Cubrio. He was also the boss of the Rinaldo Construction Company, saw cities built and wrecked while describing the actions in minute detail to the rest of us. And there were moments when he would embrace Sarah or me and beg us to have his men go away, or would fall asleep exhausted after living through the battles raging inside himself. I admired the beauty and the power of his language and the force of his fantasies and was touched by his occasional gentleness and weakness. After one of his rampages he would fall limp and sleep for hours. I remember him waking up once and telling me that it was time to declare a National Leave Rinaldo Alone Week.

Even though Tommy wasn't officially my student, I

dreamed of helping him become a poet or a builder, or just reducing his pain into livable and sharable form. I talked to him, at times held him while he broadcast declarations of war and proclamations of peace, and tried to get inside his world or to interest him in mine. But by the time I left the Reece School, I had given up on him. He seemed to me to be surrounded by doors that had no keys, by one-way windows, by empty space. Somehow he had decided not to grow but to rage on until he collapsed.

Thinking about my three students, John, Fred, and Harry, and about Tommy, reminds me of a quote I found in a collection of letters from the English poet Sir John Suckling: "And Jack, if you would make a visit to Bedlam, you shall find that there are rarely two there mad for the same thing." No two of my students were mad for the same thing. Each of them was terrified of the world and had built up a system of protection that though bizarre and sad kept him from falling to pieces completely. Harry, for example, built his life around the clock. Spelling for him was "time to clock the letters" and snacktime was "juice o'clock time." If for some reason the daily schedule changed, Harry panicked and began smashing his head with his fists while repeating, "The clock is broken, the clock is broken." I learned to take his metaphor seriously after a while and told him that I was a clock-repair specialist and knew how to fix broken clocks. When he realized I was serious, he let me repair the clock of his day and came to feel secure about living through the inevitable irregularities of daily life.

Harry had as much of an impact on me as I may have had on him. Those days I felt quite lonely and isolated, and occasionally I would find myself hitting myself in the head in frustration and watching clocks all the time. His world and his words were powerful, frightening metaphors of fragility.

John was quite different. He was sneaky and always

seemed ready to explode, but was never able to. He once told me that he was dangerous like a crab. He saw himself as a subterranean creature and used to love to lock himself in the bathroom and pretend he was devouring little children (especially his younger brother).

John was extremely strong and well coordinated, quite the opposite of Harry and Fred. His hands were strikingly large and heavy, unusually broad from the thumb to the pinkie. His appearance and bearing had a gravity and sophistication that was precocious. A superficial and short acquaintance with John would probably give one the impression of a handsome, normal, compliant youngster, strong and able to play a joke, anxious to please, and not very loud or assertive. John almost invariably fell into this pattern when he first met someone, and appeared sweet, giving, and controlled for several days at a time—until he felt sure enough of himself to begin to manipulate, control, and defy the adult, and to try to relax physically with him. But John's muscles were in a continued state of contraction and tension, and I don't think I ever saw him relaxed.

Fred provided some levity in this sad world. He wanted to be funny, to make everyone laugh and be happy, but somehow he never developed a sense of how other people felt. He would jump around, tell a joke, and then look about for some recognition that he was trying to gain. He didn't seem to know where he ended and the world began. I remember a time when he got his fingers caught in a door. He looked at me and asked, "Does it hurt?" I said no and he walked away smiling and relieved. Another day, out of what was perhaps a perverse curiosity about the nature of his feelings, I banged my fist on his desk about six inches from his hand. He looked up at me and asked the same question: "Does it hurt?" and I said yes. He burst into tears and showed obvious pain. After this incident I decided never to experiment with my students' feelings, but to try in a direct and nonmanipulative way to discuss dysfunctional behavior and support students' efforts to change their own behavior.

I remember one of the last times I saw Fred. We were walking to a mailbox near the school. He had written several letters to his grandparents and I felt it was important for him to mail them himself. When he dropped the letters in the mailbox I said good-bye to them on a whim. Harry turned to me anxiously, then paused and laughed. He said, "You made a joke, didn't you. That's what a joke is." That moment was one of the first times I felt successful as a teacher. He had grown to the point where he could deal with my intentions without any help.

Recently I came upon a report I wrote in 1961 that gives a specific sense of how my first teaching days went. Here are a few excerpts:

> The day begins ritualistically. Each student gets settled in his own way, then sits at his own table and gets ready to work. At exactly 9:00 (it would upset Harry if we began a minute before or after 9) we begin academics.
>
> Fred puts his arithmetic book on the table and awaits his assignment. He immediately gets to work when told to, but cannot start without instructions. John has a more difficult time getting settled and so I speak to him, teach him whatever is new, or set him at work on familiar material. After about 15 or 20 minutes he is settled enough for me to shift my attention to Fred and teach him new work, or what is more usual, help him with problems that require understanding as well as mechanical calculation.
>
> About 9:45 Fred finishes his arithmetic and begins spelling. He can understand directions by himself if he has come across similar ones before, but has to be eased through anything new or different. While Fred is doing spelling, John spends time practicing script writing, which he is still in the process of acquiring. Academics lasts until 10:15 or 10:25 depending upon Fred and John's ability to concentrate and work profitably. Fred is on

Book 5 in spelling and is beginning to encounter difficulty; John has some troubles in Book 3, due more to attention difficulties than to a lack of understanding.

The rest of the day went on in much the same way. There was nothing particularly interesting about the educational content of the material I was required to teach. The students, however, had such individual styles and needs that I was obliged to learn quite quickly how to change the curriculum so that it would be useful to them. John worked best with material that was visually interesting; Harry needed to learn in even more structured and organized ways than the texts we had; and Fred needed funny writing that dealt with feelings. After a few months, I found myself reworking the basic curriculum into three different curriculums, a tendency I've never lost.

My initial anxiety over teaching disturbed children disappeared with prolonged contact with the students. They eventually emerged as eleven-year-old children, somewhat different from most eleven-year-old children, with greater pain, disorientation, and confusion, but nevertheless distinct and interesting people.

6.

TEACHERS COLLEGE
AND
STUDENT TEACHING

After six months at the Reece School, I began to think about public school teaching again and about working with so-called normal children. The slow rate of change of my students depressed me. I'd see a tiny positive difference negated by a change in the weather or in the emotional constellation of the class. I saw the children's fear of change overwhelm their desire to grow. I also knew I was beginning to do kind and decent work. But it wasn't enough, was too slow, too removed from the world of lively, articulate children I wanted to work with. I kept thinking of the secretary at the New York City Board of Education and resigned myself to going to Teachers College, Columbia, and taking courses, any courses, that would get me a regular elementary school credential and a job in the public schools.

Every beginning teacher has to face similar questions: What kind of child do you want to spend five hours a day with? How many children do you like to work with at one time? What age do you enjoy being with? The central question teachers have to answer for themselves is: What kind of growth do you want to nurture?

My wife is an excellent teacher of severely disturbed children, takes pleasure in observing small increments of growth, and has the patience to see them disappear and reappear. She likes to work with small groups. I'm different. I like large groups, enjoy noise and defiance, and dramatic change. Teaching friends of mine all have their preferences: Some like to work with adolescents, some with very young children. Some change every three years in order to experience growth on different age levels. Others are subject obsessed and enjoy stimulating scientific, mathematical, literary, or historical understanding. What we all realize, however, is that our most effective teaching arises from being in a situation where the growth we nurture is something we find beautiful to witness.

My time at Teachers College dragged. I spent the summer of 1961 taking classes on the teaching of arithmetic and reading, on curriculum development (which taught us how to make our own Ditto masters), on educational counseling (which told us to be nice to children), and on children's literature (which exposed us to books which, it seemed to me then, were written to avoid exposing children to poetry and fiction that dealt with life in complex and controversial ways). My professors gave the impression that they knew how to mold one into a good teacher. All you had to do was be nice, be organized, fit into the system as it was, follow the methods you learned at Teachers College, and you'd have a long and happy career. None of it seemed right to me and so for that summer and through the fall semester when I took a full course load and did student teaching, I played bad boy and devil's advocate. I brought poet friends of mine to the children's literature course, asked impertinent questions about abstract math during a class on the teaching of times tables, raised the issue of racism in the class on individual counseling. I realized the contradiction between my wanting to be respected as a teacher and my disrespectful attitude toward my professors. Part of my attitude could be attributed to a small doubt about whether indeed a Harvard man should teach in elementary school. But there was another, more serious aspect of my questioning. The content of what was being taught to us was vacuous, the skills and techniques could have been mastered by a high school sophomore and the psychology found in any Miss Lonelyhearts column. The reality of life in the classroom, the complexity and variability of children, the effect of the school and community on the teacher, the role of culture in learning—these were never dealt with and I cannot recollect anything specific about those classes other than that they were boring. The classes I hoped to learn most from, those about the education of disturbed children, were the worst. They talked about categories of disturbance, about interventions and therapeutic strategies, and said nothing pertinent or helpful about John, Fred, or Harry.

If it wasn't for the nurturance, good sense, and eventual protection of my supervisor Dorothy McGeoch, I never would have survived Teachers College and gotten a teaching credential. Throughout my experience I have always been lucky to find one or two teachers who helped me to grow the way I came to help my students. Without those teachers and colleagues, none of us sustain a life of teaching. It makes good sense when going to a new school to take time to look for such a colleague, to find someone whom you want to learn from and share what you know with.

I had two student teacher placements instead of the more usual one. My first placement was at P.S. 140, right opposite Peter Cooper Village, a middle-class development on Manhattan's East Side. I was assigned to a well-ordered, smoothly functioning, traditional sixth-grade classroom. The day opened with reading the headlines and one article from the front page of the *New York Times* and went step by step through group reading, individualized reading, spelling, math, social studies, art—what seemed to me an endless series of disconnected lessons that students had to go through. Here were normal children doing just what my students at the Reece School were doing. At Reece it was clear that the

structure and the workbooks existed as much to control behavior as to teach anything. It hadn't occurred to me until I
had spent six weeks at P.S. 140 that the same thing was being
done to normal students. Every day was the same, every
lesson the same, every question like every other. I didn't hear
student voices except on the playground and in the lunch-
room. The teacher, Mrs. Jay, only spoke to the students about
formal matters (absence notes, parents' permission forms,
etc.) or when she gave orders or asked questions about a
lesson. I wanted to object to what I saw, to try to have conversations with my students and find out what interested them.
They looked so lively and alert on the playground. Fortunately Dorothy McGeoch convinced me to keep quiet and
do what I was told. She reminded me that my goal in student
teaching was to pass the course, not reform the school. I could
try that, she said wryly, when I got my credential and was
doing real work.

I almost survived 140. However, I made a number of
inadvertent mistakes that led to the involuntary termination
of my student teaching two weeks before it was to have
ended. The first mistake was to treat the principal informally.
I had always been able to relate to my professors and colleagues at the Reece School on a first-name basis and didn't
realize that formal address was required in exchanges between student teachers and staff and administration.

Another mistake was fraternizing with students. I said
hello to every youngster I passed on the street, in the yard, or
in the hall. After a while some children began asking me
questions about myself or telling me the neighborhood or
school gossip. I didn't realize it made the other teachers as
well as the administrators around the school angry to see me
chatting with the students, and it wasn't until I left the school
that another student teacher told me that the principal had
held me up as an example of how a teacher should not behave.
He informed the other teachers at the school that eating lunch

with the students and playing with them on breaks instead of
having coffee in the teachers' room was unprofessional behavior that contributed to the breakdown of discipline and
respect and could not be allowed in an orderly school.

Mrs. Jay, my supervising teacher, didn't like to have me
in the room. I was too arrogant toward her, an attitude that I
now see as foolish and one that may well have kept me from
learning from her. She contrived to have me work with a
small number of her "slower and difficult" students in a small
conference room down the hall. I was given four students—
Stanley Gold, the biggest and oldest boy in the school, who it
turned out was half Jewish and half Puerto Rican; Betty Wil-
liams, who was black; Robert Moy, who was Chinese and had
recently arrived in the country; and Ana Suarez, who was
Puerto Rican. With one exception, they were the only minority children in the class of thirty-five.

When I first heard of the arrangement, it felt like being
demoted to the Reece School—one teacher and four deviant
youngsters. However, it proved to be a gift. I couldn't have
learned more about children, culture, and learning in such a
short time than I did from working with those four lively,
intelligent, defiant, and thoroughly delightful youngsters.

As soon as we left the classroom the four came alive, chatted about what was going on, asked me about myself, particularly why I wanted to be a teacher. Once I sat down to read
with them, some unexpected things began to happen. Betty
didn't know the alphabet, or even how to hold a pencil. I
asked her how long she'd been in school, since everything
about formal learning seemed so foreign to her. She told me
that this was her first year, that she had come from a small
farm community in the South where the children didn't go to
school much. When Betty first came to school in September,
there was a suggestion she be put in the first grade, but that
was abandoned because she was so tall. She spent her time in

the sixth grade in the back of the room, flipping through picture books.

Betty was my first teaching success. I taught her how to hold a pencil, read stories to her and had her copy them, gave her flash cards using words she wanted to know, and watched her learn to read. She wasn't dumb or a failure—just a child who hadn't learned to read and was learning at twelve, not a bad age to begin formal reading instruction.

Working with Betty showed me the futility of trying to teach reading solely through phonics. Betty grew up in the Deep South, and she and I simply didn't pronounce *a, e, i, o* and *u* in the same way. In fact, between my Bronx accent and her Southern accent, there were few words that sounded identical to us. The meaning of sentences and the content of stories, however, made it easy to overcome these differences. Betty and I spoke about books and understood each other perfectly. The more we talked about books, the more interested she became in reading well. Our lessons were planned around questions she raised about reading. I began to realize that she was my best source of information about teaching her to read. As long as she could specify what caused her reading problems, I could help her. If endings like *-ion* or *-ally* were a problem, I could simply tell her how they were used and pronounced. If combinations like *-oa-* or *-ae-* or *-ea-* created confusion, it was easy to undo them as long as she could point to them. Through teaching Betty and the other three youngsters that were assigned to me, I learned how to use students' knowledge of their own learning problems as a major source for designing educational programs.

Betty's mother met me one day after school. She told me that Betty was very happy about learning to read and she wondered if I could give her materials so Betty could practice more at home. In her eyes I was a real teacher, though I knew I was only improvising. Nevertheless, I bought six inexpensive simple reading books at a remainder bookstore, six pencils and a pencil sharpener, a notebook and a pack of three-by-five index cards, and packaged them in a plastic box with Betty's name stenciled on it. That was her personalized reading kit and from what I heard several years later from another student, she had used it and taught herself to read.

Robert Moy, another one of my four, also fascinated me. I tried to administer a Gates Reading Test to find out his level and gave up one-fourth of the way through. He couldn't read any English, could hardly pronounce the sounds of the language. There was a math section on the test and I tried that since there was no reason to assume he couldn't do math because he couldn't read English. He scored 100 percent or the equivalent of twelfth-grade level in math. A few days later I gave him an eighth-grade math test and he scored in the ninety-ninth percentile, yet in class he was in a fourth-grade workbook because he couldn't read the verbalized math problems. I remember feeling at the time that the main difference between the Reece School and P.S. 140 was that in 140 the adults were doing crazy things to sane children instead of the other way around.

I noticed some Chinese writing on Robert's book and asked him if he wrote Chinese. Yes, he knew over a thousand characters and would be delighted to teach them to me. I shared my discovery about Robert's writing ability with my supervising teacher and she made a note of it, to use, as she told me, during the China unit she was planning for the second half of the school year. She didn't say anything to Robert. I watched as he systematically went about learning bits and pieces of English. He may not have been well schooled at 140, but somewhere he had been educated well. He just needed to be pointed in the right direction and given a few basic instructions in order to learn to read skillfully.

The students I got closest to in that class were Ana Suarez and Stanley Gold. Neither had a reading or a math problem.

Older than the other students, they were leaders in the small ghetto a few blocks from the school, and had no relationship with most of the students in P.S. 140, which was at that time over 80 percent white. The teachers, they claimed, didn't like them and so they "refused to do any work, period," as Stanley said.

I brought Ana romances and gothics, which she loved. After learning that Stanley's father was a woodcarver and Stanley a talented artist, I got him some art instruction books. That was my first reading class—Betty copying Dr. Seuss, Robert teaching me Chinese, Ana reading romances and talking endlessly about the story, while Stanley drew and read about art.

After three weeks Ana's little sister Maria came to me after school and said their mother and father wanted to invite me to lunch on Saturday. I accepted though I had no idea why the invitation was made. It turned out Stanley's mother, Ana's parents, and a few other parents had been watching my work and felt I cared about their children. They knew my tenure at the school would be brief and wanted to pump me about how their children were being treated. The lunch, which stretched through dinner and well into the evening, was wonderful. It was the first Puerto Rican food I'd eaten and was a delicious new cuisine to explore. The more I praised Gertrude's cooking in my broken Spanish (she spoke no English at all, though her children were fully bilingual), the more new dishes appeared on the table. We talked about school for a few hours, then some people joined us, some beer was passed around, musical instruments appeared, there was music, dinner, more talk about schools, and an invitation to return the next Friday for a really special dinner.

I became friends with the Suarez family and with Stanley's mother and remained friends for years. In fact, when I got married three years later, Rafael, Ana's father, was the musician at the wedding. Fraternizing with parents has been one of the joys of my teaching life. It has also given me roots in the communities I serve and makes it easy to ask people to help me teach their children.

My extracurricular relationship with Stanley Gold, however, was what led directly to my being removed from 140. Stanley and I prepared an art project to present to Mrs. Jay's class during the morning I would be expected to run the whole class by myself. Mrs. Jay would evaluate my student teaching on the basis of the math, language, and art lessons presented then. I decided to put math and art together and do a lesson on how cathedrals stand up. I was intoxicated with the cathedrals I'd seen in France, and Stanley had shown me pictures of carved models of churches his father had made. For the lesson, Stanley was going to draw on the chalkboard a schematic of a cathedral with flying buttresses and then do a scale drawing of Chartres that compared it in size with the school and the Empire State Building. The math component of the lesson was an introduction to scale and relative proportion. The whole thing was to take up the first hour of class time. The lesson couldn't have worked, but I didn't know it. The class wasn't prepared for an open-ended discussion about anything, much less about flying buttresses; the math was too sophisticated; I had no experience working with a whole class and no sense of how to maintain control. To make matters worse, that day Mrs. Jay was absent and a sub appeared at the door at eight-forty. Stanley and I had been in the room since eight o'clock, he drawing on the board and I setting up the materials for my other lessons. The sub looked at Mrs. Jay's lesson book and let me take over.

The class came in and settled down. I began talking about the plans for the morning and then asked if anyone knew what a cathedral was. Six hands went up, three people shouted, someone made a strange noise. If Mrs. Jay was there, none of that would have happened, and it might have been possible for me to rescue part of the lesson because of the control her presence exerted. But with a sub in the room, I got more loudness than openness. After fifteen minutes the sub walked to the front of the room, banged a ruler on the desk, and in an experienced voice informed the class that she not only knew how to maintain order but demanded it instantly. She got her silence and then turned to Stanley, then to the buttressed church on the board, and commanded, "Erase that." He refused, she commanded again, and Stanley turned to me and asked if I was going to make him erase it. I saw our whole relationship dissolving, felt the possibility of his withdrawing from me as he did from all his other teachers, and I turned to the sub, saying something like "It stays." She then commanded me to erase the board. I refused and she stormed out of the room.

Somehow I fumbled through what was left of my lesson plans until recess. After my class left the room, the principal came in and told me to take the rest of the day off.

When I returned the next day, there was a note taped to my locker in the student teacher's lounge, informing me to go to the principal's office. The locker was emptied of all my books and materials, which the principal later presented to me in a neatly sealed box while instructing me that I was never to return to P.S. 140 again, for any reason. I had violated the sacred law of the teaching profession: Never under any circumstances support a student against another teacher in the presence of students. I was not even allowed to say good-bye to the class.

Halfway out of the building, I started crying quietly. It felt as if I was being sent away from home, from what I loved more than anything else. The place, the children, the energy, the best and the worst of that school, all of a sudden were precious, and now I would never get my credential and be part of it.

Dorothy McGeoch rescued me. She somehow managed to bury the principal's report and get me assigned to Walden

School, a small progressive private school on Central Park West. However, every moment I could manage was spent with Stanley or the Suarez family and their friends in the neighborhood of P.S. 140.

A number of things impressed me during my brief stay at Walden. Children can be self-governing at an early age and can learn well without being pushed, manipulated, or controlled. The Walden primary school was beautiful. I had never seen Cuisinaire rods or Montessori and other manipulative materials before. Play and learning weren't separate in my life, but Walden showed me how the two could work together in a school setting.

The upper grades, however, seemed as dismal to me as the primary grades seemed wonderful. The setting was informal. There was no physical punishment or reward system. Teachers and students were on a first-name basis. Yet I sensed that the students were being psychologically manipulated and often punished by their teachers. I remember a particular case where a boy didn't want to participate in a quiet activity. He wanted to run around, talk, perhaps sing or dance. His teacher came over to him and said, "You don't want to run around, do you?" The boy's answer was "Yes," to which the teacher responded, "What's troubling you today?" I began to witness a minitherapy session which seemed all wrong to me. The youngster wanted to do something loud but positive and was being treated as a neurotic who had to be brought into line. It seemed to me that it would have been sounder for the teacher simply to admit (as was the case) that the staff insisted upon an hour's quiet work during the day instead of trying to manipulate the student into accepting something he was opposed to. I believe in being direct and clear about your intentions and reasons, and letting children know why you're acting the way you are. In the Walden case, the problem was that the teachers wanted to coerce the students into an hour of silence but their philosophy was opposed to coercion. The only way they found to overcome that contradiction was to resort to psychological manipulation. Fortunately my student teaching ended before I had a chance to express my feelings about this to the staff, or else I probably never would have gotten through Teachers College.

7.

THE PUBLIC SCHOOLS
AT LAST

When I finally obtained my credential and got hired at P.S. 145 in February 1962, it seemed a long journey had ended. My calling to teach had been confirmed and I was ready to practice my craft behind the doors of my own classroom.

I had begun to get an idea of how I would like to see a classroom function. Conversation would be essential, for students must have a chance to talk about what they were studying and about their lives as well. The teacher would be part of the conversation, more informed about issues of content but also a listener and a learner. The students shouldn't all have to do the same thing at the same moment and shouldn't always have to be watched. Life in the classroom should be more like life at home or in a restaurant, a playground, or any place where activity occurred without constant surveillance. This implied that I would allow the students to be independent so that they would not feel at war with me and the school.

Small-group learning, individual projects, class discussions and events, and fun were some of the ingredients I wanted to develop in my work. I also wished to incorporate interesting content, compelling reading and drama, exciting math and science ideas and experiments, historical explorations and recreations, even philosophy. I also wanted to mix the subjects together—to study light, for example, from a perspective that was artistic, scientific, and literary.

To teach this way, some classroom reorganization, in terms of space, time, and behavior, would be necessary, but the specifics of how to create an open classroom were very vague to me. I had never seen or read about a working model of that kind of learning, a situation I now find ironical, given that my M.A. in education is from Teachers College, where such models were created and refined from the 1920s to the 1950s. I sometimes wonder how much finer a teacher I might have been if my degree was taken in '42 instead of '62.

I began my career in P.S. 145 with a sense of how I'd like to encourage the growth of my students but with no sense of the specifics of organization, management, discipline, pacing, and transformation of interesting content into a challenging curriculum. My strengths were energy, enthusiasm, knowledge in many different areas, a love of books and learning, a delight in being in the presence of children, an almost fanatic determination not to fail as a teacher, and a faith in my fifth-grade students' ability to learn no matter how limited they seemed when I first encountered them. My class had managed to wear out half a dozen teachers by the time I took over in February. A third of them spoke only Spanish, the class itself was a dumping ground for problem students, and there were no books in the room. No matter—I was full of confidence, even of a sense of destiny.

My first week of teaching left me in despair, almost wishing I'd finished my doctorate in philosophy and could teach Wittgenstein to a group of docile graduate students. The first mistake I made was to introduce myself to the class as Herb instead of Mr. Kohl. I had done so at Walden and it seemed like a good idea. But twenty blocks away at P.S. 145, the only adults you called by their first names were those you didn't respect and were trying to bait. In one short week I went from informal Herb, with an open collar and sweater, to Mr. Kohl, with a suit and tie, a very controlled manner, and an unnatural stern look. My students had quickly taught me that I had to establish my authority before I could teach them anything.

In fact, after several weeks I found myself doing everything I had sworn never to do in the classroom. The day began with students copying something I'd written on the chalkboard. After that they'd fill in purple Ditto forms with simple math examples, then read out loud, then go to recess and repeat the process. In my heart I wanted to talk to my students, to share what I knew with them and find out who they were and what they knew. Yet all I was doing was filling up time and trying to get through the day without a scene.

Yet there were scenes—fights, thefts, furniture overturned or thrown around, papers torn up, pencils broken. Occasionally there were moments when one student or another did start a conversation with me or follow a suggestion I had made or, most wonderful, look happy and relaxed in the room. I took to studying faces and gestures in ways I'd never done before. Every moment of silence in the room was a time for me to observe, to guess (usually wildly and incorrectly) about who these children were who were forced to be with me five hours a day.

After a while little things happened that made our lives together better. Vincent made a joke about my hair and I laughed. Gloria said that teachers don't laugh, so I couldn't be a real teacher. Another time, Carlos told me that the reason Victor was so shy in class was that he had just come from Puerto Rico and couldn't speak any English. I asked Carlos to be my interpreter and set aside twenty minutes a day for my students to teach me Spanish, even though my principal told me that speaking Spanish in class was against Board of Education rules. Little by little I felt that I was becoming myself in the classroom and abandoning my stance as the Teacher.

One girl's mother had a back injury and was in traction in the hospital. She was from Puerto Rico and couldn't eat the institutional American-style food served her in the ward. Her family was worried about her health. She was weak and hungry and her back wasn't getting any better. One lunchtime, her daughter Rafaela, who was one of the few quiet children in my classroom, asked me if I would do her a favor. She wanted me to sneak *pasteles* and other tasty Puerto Rican food to her mother at the hospital. It would fit in my briefcase, she said, and no one would question a teacher.

Why did she ask me? I wondered if she picked up something that first inept day when I introduced myself as Herb. More likely, she was desperate and I was the only one left to turn to. Whatever the reason, the day I visited the hospital I had the best-smelling briefcase you can imagine and Consuelo, Rafaela's mother, had a wonderful dinner.

Everyone in the class knew I'd broken the hospital rules, did something they thought was dangerous, and didn't ask for any money or other return. They began to open up because of that and other gestures that led them, as they later told me, to like being in class. They'd appreciated my making pencils available for children who couldn't afford them, allowing them to pass notes if it didn't interfere with anything, giving them time to talk before work began, providing colored paper for them to cover their books with, letting them take home books and games I brought to school, and trusting them to be able to run the film-strip viewer by themselves.

One of my ways of relating to them got me in trouble again. I had maintained my habit of saying hello to every student I met and of stopping to chat with students before and after school. One day the principal called me into his office and delivered the familiar reprimand that I was getting too close to students, and that it was undermining their respect for me. My experience, I said, was that the opposite was true, that those small gestures of friendship and concern were the basis for genuine respect. An older teacher who had over-heard our conversation told me at lunch that I'd never last at that school.

It was true that one could hardly tell from my students' unruly behavior during class that we were beginning to know and care about each other. But before and after class were different. Students came early and stayed after school to talk with me, the same students, often, who acted most defiantly and crazily during the school day.

The two notable ones were James T. and Felipe, whom the rest of the class called the Dynamic Duo, after Batman and Robin. There were days when I felt that I was in a match against the Duo, with the rest of the class as audience and judge. I didn't want to win it, but I couldn't lose, either, if I was to be of any use to the whole class. How was I to end this confrontation without victors or vanquished, without loss of face on anyone's part? I was encountering the central problem of discipline in the classroom.

James T. and Felipe were veterans of school wars and knew dozens of strategies that effectively demoralized their teachers. I knew that the problems they created had to be solved within the classroom, not by the principal's office. For-tunately the two boys were as interesting as any children I've known, and when I got home after school and thought about the day, I would have to laugh at how smart they were about taking control of the class away from me. Unlike the children at the Reece School, they knew what they were doing, and could talk their way out of the havoc they created. When it suited them, they could also be serious, intelligent, and sensi-tive. But for a while, having fun at my expense was their main game.

One Monday, for example, I was preaching to the class about how important it was to study animal life. I had bought a fifty-gallon aquarium over the weekend and brought it to class. My idea was to have goldfish, guppies, and algae eaters to study, as well as water plants and perhaps some snails. James T. and Felipe listened attentively for a change. When the bell rang for lunch, the Dynamic Duo gathered a few other boys and two girls, Gloria and Haydee, who always ran with their gang. They were talking excitedly about fish and aquariums. I couldn't make out what they were saying, for it was a mixture of English, Spanish, and Haitian French. At lunchtime the whole bunch asked to borrow the class waste-baskets and then took off. I knew something was up because they had left their lunches behind in the classroom.

I found out what the gang had in mind when I returned from lunch and almost slipped on the water that was flooding out of our aquarium. A stream was heading under the door and probably down the hall toward the principal's office. The aquarium was overflowing, the four faucets of our two blocked-up sinks were on full force, and in the aquarium and the two sinks were dozens of overgrown goldfish, actually carp, that the gang had caught in the wastebaskets on their fast trip to a nearby pond in Central Park.

The smallest fish was six inches, the largest could have been close to two feet. The fish were too big for the sinks or the aquarium; several were flapping around on the floor, gasping for air. James T. and Felipe turned to me, beaming, and said, "See, Mr. Kohl, you don't need to buy no fish. We took care of it."

At that point, Gloria, Haydee, Josi, and John came into the class with a garbage can filled with yet more carp. They told me they had dumped the can's contents in front of some rich apartment house because they had people there who always cleaned up the garbage. I didn't know whether to blow up or laugh, to resign my job or congratulate the class for stocking the aquarium, and try to cover for them and myself. I simply did not know what to do. Felipe rescued me. He told me not to worry, that all the dead and big fish would be taken home and eaten. James T. added that it would be a whole system, just like I was talking about in the morning. Nothing would be wasted.

I managed to get through the afternoon, but have no idea how. We ended up with an aquarium that contained three greedy seven- or eight-inch-long carp that ate bits and scraps of everything including the few guppies and goldfish I foolishly tried to introduce.

In a way the aquarium was like our class. Several large fish overwhelming all the others and a teacher who, though bigger than the students, was always on the verge of being eaten up by the class.

James T. and Felipe were the kind of children who some cynical educators would classify as hyperactive, educationally handicapped, retarded, disturbed, learning disabled, and so forth. They were all of these in class, and in their lives none of these. They hated school, had experienced five and a half years of bad teaching and acted out their hostility to stay sane in an insane situation. I watched them grow, from tossing books around the classroom to sneaking looks at them and by June asking me for help in reading after school. They changed slowly, yet compared to the children at the Reece School, they seemed to be leaping forward.

James T. turned out to be a very skilled artist. He told me that when he saw colors he could taste them in his mouth, and I once caught him dipping his fingers in our tempera paints and licking them. I surprised him one day by giving him a box of pastels. I made up some story that the school was providing special art material to students of talent to help decorate the halls. James T. made several beautiful pastel drawings. A particular favorite of mine (which I still have) is a drawing of Moby Dick on black construction paper. The black underlies the pastel white whale, deep blue water, and pale blue sky, giving the whole an appropriately ominous feeling.

I mounted a number of James T.'s pastels on poster board and hung them in the hall. This got me in trouble several weeks later when the district art supervisor came into my class and in front of the students told me to take down James T.'s posters. I remembered what had happened to me with the sub in 140 and decided to stall. I muttered something that could have been taken for assent, but explained that we were about to take an important phonics test. By this time I'd learned that phonics always takes preference over any other matter.

The supervisor didn't give up easily on the pastels and was waiting in my classroom when I returned from dismissing the class. The assistant principal accompanied her. Lois was a very sympathetic woman who protected her teachers. I could see James T. and Felipe hiding behind the swinging doors down the hall. The supervisor advised me that pastels were a sixth-grade medium and that since I was teaching fifth grade, my students couldn't use pastels. She showed me a passage in the school district's art curriculum manual that confirmed her contention and insisted again that the offending art be removed. She also wanted to confiscate the pastels in my room. I politely objected, pointing out that the 5-1 class, of so-called gifted students (my class was 5-7, the bottom of our grade), used pastels. My motivation was to show my students and particularly James T. that he could do work that was as good as or better than that of some of the students in 5-1. She said that the only reason 5-1 was allowed to use pastels was that they all read and did math on a sixth-grade or better level. By now I was getting angry and was about to argue that art and reading skills had no direct relationship, that the development of any skill could lead to confidence in other areas, that there was no set sequence of the use of art materials, that . . . Lois put her hand on my shoulder and shrugged. Her eyes told me what I quickly realized. We were in an educational madhouse and my students and I would be the losers if I protested any further. James T.'s work came down. The supervisor even demanded that I turn over the pastels, but since they were not the brand bought by the school I was able to keep them.

James T. and Felipe burst into the room when my visitors had left. They wanted to know why I had given in and accused me of not caring about them. James T. picked up the box of pastels and carefully selected one of his favorite colors, a deep red, and broke it. Before he could destroy the set, I grabbed it and told him it was mine, not the school's, and he couldn't treat my property that way. I also told him that the drawings had to come down or I'd be fired; it was as simple as that. I wanted to stay with the class, not be fired, and would hang them up in the classroom if it was okay with the assistant principal. He could also keep the pastels and use them in class; they were a gift. He said he'd think about it and the two of them left.

That night I couldn't plan my lessons, and so I went downtown to visit the Suarezes and told them about the madness of the afternoon. Gertrude told me not to worry and assured me that all my students knew how crazy school was and would be interested in knowing I was a victim too. Her husband, Rafael, ended the conversation with the remark: "And it will help you too."

He was right. The next morning James T. and Felipe were waiting for me at the classroom door. James T. had drawn an elaborate sheriff's badge, which Felipe presented to me. It said: "Honorary Student."

Felipe could make leaps like that. His mind and his temperament were poetic. I liked to play language games with the class when they were under control. There was one particular exercise where students had to do variations on the metaphor "He had a heart of gold" by using the form:

_____ had a _____ of _____

  [name]   [body   [animal/
                    part]   vegetable/
                                  mineral]

Typical responses were:
> She had a heart of stone.
> He had a head of rocks.
> He had a fist of steel.

Felipe's responses were:
> James T. has a finger of yellow blood.
> Gloria has a half face of gold and another half face of angry.

James T. loved yellow and occasionally used his finger to apply yellow tints to some of his work. Gloria was well known for being two-faced—sweet, kind, fickle, and dangerous.

James T. and Felipe weren't the only children who taught me how to teach them and gave me hints about what interested ten- and eleven-year-olds. One day Lilian, one of the few quiet children, was looking through my salesman's case that I kept full of learning materials. Carrying the case to school had become a habit after a few weeks at 145, when I realized how much children love to discover new things without having to be told they must learn about them. The case usually contained books, magazines, games, magnets, magnifying glasses, free samples, newspapers—anything I thought might interest the class. The children were allowed to look through it and borrow something after they had handed their finished work in to me and waited while I graded it. That day Lilian came upon a blueprint of one of my father's old jobs, which I had asked for. She spread the blueprint on the floor and began puzzling out what was on it. Carlos Gomez, whose father was the janitor of a large apartment house, immediately recognized it as the floor plan of a building. His father had taught him a bit about blueprint reading and he attracted a crowd of about a dozen admiring classmates as he revealed the mysteries of architectural drawing to Lilian.

Carlos was usually quiet and studious. He always finished his work quickly, always asked for more, never wanted to pause and chat. This was the liveliest I'd seen him, and watching the scene in the back of the room caused me to wonder what was locked up in all the children, what they knew and could contribute. How to find out? How to do so when so much of my energy went into controlling them and filling in forms and doing workbooks just to get through the day in moderate peace?

I taped the blueprint to the blackboard and explained that my father was a builder. Vincent asked if he would come to visit the class. Gloria wanted to know if he was better looking than I was. It was almost three o'clock and so instead of explaining at length, I described the function of a blueprint and assigned the students the task of drawing a blueprint of their apartments for homework. It was the most successful assignment I'd given so far.

When the students brought their assignments in the next day, it was clear that something special had happened. Just about everyone had drawn a coherent representation of where they lived. A number of students had got help from brothers and sisters. Some used top-down perspective, others mixed different perspectives; different labeling systems were invented. We spent the entire morning looking over the drawings and talking about them. Many of the children knew each other's apartments and picked up on a missing window or misplaced chair or table. We concluded the discussion by drawing floor plans of the classroom.

The morning was one of the few I experienced at 145 that gave me a glimpse of what a good classroom could be like. If I had been more experienced, it would have been possible to follow up and develop a more extended curriculum revolving about building construction, model making, scale drawing, and symbol systems in general. But the burden of daily routine, the fear that reading, writing, and arithmetic wouldn't be adequately mastered if I followed the students' interests and planned around them, and the simple fact that learning to

Richard

OUTLINE OF MY HOME.

19. SMALL CABINET.
20. BICURBO
21. BED
22. BED.
23. BICURRO
24. SMALL TABLE
25. CLOSET.
26. HALL.
27. OUTSIDE DOOR.

1. RADIO HIGH FI.
2. SOFA
3. CHAIRS
4. TV.
5. CHAIR
6. BUREO
7. BED
8. SMALL CABINET.
9. CLOSET.

10. TUB.
11. TOILET BOLE.
12. MEDICINE CHEST.
13. CABINET (DISHES).
14. STOVE
15. SINK
16. WASHING MACHINE
17. TABLE.
18. BED

teach was exhausting work that left little time to research and plan, sent me back to my usual routine the next day.

But by June the first two hours of the morning were won. We talked and read together. I took my Spanish lesson. We discussed history, science and art. No one acted too disruptively. The last hour of the morning was a strain on all of us. It was my most rigid time of day, and whenever possible I extended recess and left for lunch early.

The students won the afternoon. By one o'clock I was too exhausted to entertain, discipline, or teach the class. But eventually this time became fun for all of us. They could paint, draw, sculpt, watch the fish, do science experiments, read or do math, get individual help from me, listen to music and occasionally dance. The only conditions were that they couldn't fight (they did occasionally) and they had to put everything away and clean up before three (they didn't occasionally). Contrary to my fears when I agreed to let the students have the afternoon to themselves, they didn't all paint the whole time, or sit filing their nails, or argue. Some students chose to do math, others science or reading, as well as art. The art itself became increasingly interesting and I began to bring in books on techniques and set them problems. The students used me too—asked for help, for resources and ideas. I still felt guilty about these "loose" afternoons, but they provided an important stage in learning how to maintain control without being coercive and how to teach skills in a creative and informal context.

June was the best teaching time I'd ever had and I was already looking forward to September. In one of the final faculty meetings, the principal gave a talk about how he wanted an open exchange between himself and the staff and asked if anyone had any comments on the school's reading program. There was silence in the room. One teacher yawned, the others kept their eyes away from the principal and their hands down. But I raised my hand and went on about how there was no coherent reading program at the school and offered ideas I'd heard or read about that could help our students. The principal smiled and thanked me for my input, but his eyes made it clear that I should have kept my mouth shut. The woman sitting next to me, an older teacher who had been very helpful to me in my first two months, whispered, "You won't be here next year."

She was right, of course. I was involuntarily transferred out of P.S. 145 with the feeling that I was being thrown out of a garden I'd worked on just as the blooming season was beginning and before the ripening of the fruits.

8.

HOW THE POLICE
DROVE ME TO
BECOMING A PRINCIPAL

Two days after school ended, I got a call from Felipe's father. His nephew and several other boys I knew had been arrested for loitering and disturbing the peace. They were being sent to Youth House and it might be weeks before they would come to trial. I later discovered that it was common for the police to arrest a few youngsters after school ended as a warning to the other kids to stay in line during the summer.

I went to see Felipe's father and talked about helping Juan and the other boys. Three of my students—Felipe, Gloria, and Vincent—were sitting on the stoop of the building and they seemed delighted to see me. I asked them what they were planning for the summer and they said "Nothing." Impulsively I offered to come by a few days a week and do some reading with them. They jumped at the opportunity and asked if they could bring along their brothers and sisters. I said fine, not realizing that the three of them had eleven brothers and sisters between the ages of four and fifteen who would volunteer to join us.

Several days later, after getting Juan and the other boys out of Youth House on the basis of a letter I wrote, using my authority as a teacher at their school (which officially I no longer was), I met my fifteen pupils, some of them for the first time. They ranged from Gloria's sister Tita, who was four and already as energetic and defiant as Gloria, to Vincent's older brother Julio, who was fifteen and couldn't read the alphabet but was a gifted painter. The group also brought along Alice, a severely retarded eight-year-old whom Gloria's family looked after. Alice couldn't speak very well, had never been to school, but she was one of us.

My plan was to take my little school to the children's book section of the Teachers College library and use TC's books, since I didn't have enough for fifteen children and was still a matriculated M.A. student in the Department of Special Education. We managed to stuff ourselves in two shifts into my Ford Falcon and arrived at TC. The children became quiet and apprehensive as soon as they left the security of their neighborhood.

The TC library was as good as a toy store for the children. There were hundreds of picture books, adventure stories, encyclopedias, sports tales. There was a book for everyone. I suggested that Julio pick a pretty alphabet book and read it with Alice. Since neither of them could read, it seemed like a sensible match-up. It just might be possible to help Julio learn to read by having him teach Alice. And it would be good for her, since Julio had immediately struck me as a patient person who was very comfortable around young children.

Everyone eventually chose a book and found a place in the library. I wandered from child to child, helping them with words or letters, answering their questions but mostly reminding them that it was important for them to keep their voices down so that the other people in the library could concentrate on their reading.

At the end of our second week in the library I was called aside by the chief librarian and told that we couldn't use it anymore. She explained that the library, though it was full of children's books, was not for children. Teachers attending classes at TC used the books and many of them had complained about the presence of children. After all, teachers have enough of children during the school year and need some peace and quiet over the summer.

Several days before, I'd read in the *New York Times* a report of a speech by the president of Teachers College, stressing the need for the university to relate to the urban community. In my time I hadn't seen much relating and now the sixteen of us from the urban community were facing expulsion from the TC library. I resolved to speak to the president and get his approval for us to use the library. It was my first political act in the field of education. All sixteen of us marched into Dr. Fisher's office. When I asked for an appointment to see him, his secretary said he was tied up for the day. I said that we'd all wait. I would have done just about anything to keep that little, informal, unfunded school together for the summer. It was my palette, my opportunity to teach and be with children, with no institutional constraints.

The president's reception room was quickly transformed by the children. Alice and Julio were sitting on the floor looking at the pictures in a *National Geographic*, Gloria and her sister Tita were going through the other secretary's desk, and Felipe and Juan were making telephone calls to all their friends. The secretary was getting quite agitated and I felt sorry about putting her in such a threatening situation. But I wanted that school bad. After about a half hour, the secretary left and then returned with Dr. Fisher. He would be delighted to talk with me if only I'd clear the office. I said I couldn't do that, there was no place to send the kids. He wanted to know what group we represented and what our demands were. I could tell that he saw us as a bigger deal than we were. All we wanted, I explained, was a room, some books, a chance to use the resources of TC just as he had suggested in his speech. The children were the community he was talking about, I concluded, and it was his responsibility to do something about it.

I was thoroughly surprised when in fact he did do something for us and was quite generous about it. We were given a room, free copies of books and tests and reading materials published by the TC press, and the services of one student in a community education class. In fact, we were even declared a community education project and people came to visit our little room and observe this project, supposedly initiated by TC, that related to the needs of poor and minority students. I was annoyed by this co-optation of my work, but kept quiet. Why not let TC take the credit? After all, it did support the work.

One major thing I learned that summer was how important students were as teaching resources. By late August, every child was both student and teacher, even Alice, who had learned enough of the alphabet from Julio to go through an alphabet picture book with four-year-old Tita.

I had to leave my little school in September, when the children returned to P.S. 145 and I had to begin again at a new school and face a new class of thirty-six children I didn't yet know. However, I can still see those children at TC and remember specific instances of their growth. For me, recalling my teaching experience is a lot like recalling the early years of my own children's growth. I forget the smelly diapers, sleepless nights, and temper tantrums, and remember their first steps and words, the first jokes they ever told, their early relationship to our pets. Such selective amnesia is probably a healthy faculty for anyone who cares to sustain a life of teaching.

PART II
THE CRAFT OF TEACHING

9.

TEACHING

SENSIBILITY

My dream of becoming a teacher was complicated by the concrete demands of teaching five hours a day five days a week. At the end of my first year in the classroom, I knew that it was possible to teach well, provided you made the effort to learn what you needed to know and do. My sense of calling began to be informed and solidified by a sense of the need for craft.

The craft of teaching has a number of aspects. It relates to the organization of content and the structuring of space and time so that learning will be fostered. It requires an understanding of students' levels of sophistication and the modes of learning they are accustomed to using. But most centrally, the craft of teaching requires what can be called teaching sensibility. This sensibility develops over a career of teaching and has to do with knowing how to help students focus their energy on learning and growth. What I mean by energy is close to what is more usually referred to as student "potential," but it's not quite that. Potential, I suppose, refers to what can be instead of what actually is at a given moment. When teachers say a student isn't "working up to potential," they mean that he isn't accomplishing something he should be. When students are described as having little or no potential, they are presumed to be incapable of learning things that more "gifted" students can. This conviction that there are clear levels and limits on what it is possible to achieve is exactly what good teachers resist. One cannot look into children's souls and see the extent and limits of their potential. Potential is not located in any part of the brain or in any organ. We don't know what people (ourselves included) could become, and any limit on expectations will become a limit on learning. That is why I choose to think of energy instead of potential. The model is fluid—energy flows, it can be expended or renewed, latent or active, it can be transformed from one form or manifestation to another. It exists in all areas of life, the emotional and physical as well as the intellectual and artistic. All youngsters have this energy, and a substantial part of the craft of teaching consists of knowing how to tap into children's energy sources or removing impediments to their flow.

This requires a feel for the way students will respond to your challenges as well as an ability to respond quickly and positively to theirs.

Teaching sensibility can be illuminated by considering how effective teachers function. I'd like to focus on one whose work I've known for years, Ron Jones. Ron taught English and coached basketball at Cubberly High School in Palo Alto. He worked with a number of free schools in the late 1960s and early 1970s, founded and still runs the Zephyrus Education Exchange, and now is program director of the Recreational Center for the Handicapped in San Francisco as well as coach of the center's Special Olympics basketball team. He also wrote *The Acorn People* and *The Wave,* which describe some of his teaching experiments.

Ron spent two weeks several years ago at a summer school that I put together every year in Point Arena, California. The school is meant to be a laboratory for teachers, a place where they can be free of the constraints of the systems they work within. It is also meant to perform the same functions for the seventy children (my own three included) who attend the school.

Ron arrived with his wife, Deanna, and his daughter, Hilary, who was six and became our youngest student. Their station wagon was loaded with rubber inner tubes, bicycle tires, Indian clubs, rope, rolls of plastic, Frisbees, and a hundred other playful, useful things. Ron reminded me of my father-in-law, a retired machinist, who always travels with his tool kit. I asked Ron why he had brought so much stuff and he said that you never knew what might come up when you worked with kids.

Ron is a quiet, unassuming person whose short sandy hair, bald spot, conservative informal dress, and middle height and weight make him seem almost a parody of ordinariness. He isn't aggressive, though he has incredible strength when tested. Students who are used to intimidating their teachers or who bully weaker students learn quickly that Ron won't tolerate cruelty. They also learn that he's incapable of being cruel himself. He's a skilled and imaginative disciplinarian who knows how to stop disruption without resorting to punishment. For example, the first day of school, Ron found himself in the middle of a fight over whether you could steal in softball. Ricky, the biggest and oldest boy at school, had already stolen bases over the objection of the rest of the youngsters, including those who were acting as umpires. When Ron came on the scene, Ricky was threatening to keep the bat and ball unless everyone else accepted his rules. Several boys turned to Ron and asked for help. Ron responded by picking up the bat and ball and commented that he'd seen softball games where you could steal and others where you couldn't, but he'd never seen any where some players could and others couldn't. He then took out a coin and told everyone that heads meant everyone can steal, tails meant nobody steals. Then he let Ricky toss it and when it came up tails not even Ricky could object. Ron had respected Ricky's seniority in the group by letting him toss the coin. Ricky wasn't punished for trying to control the rules, but he wasn't allowed to control them, either. He was given a face-saving way to refocus his energies into being part of the group. Ron then faded out of sight as the game went on.

Ron fades like that a lot. He quietly initiates an activity or deals with a problem, and then steps aside and lets learning happen. His personal presence creates trust. He approaches everything quietly, a contrast to my own louder and more aggressive style. One day everyone was gathered on our outdoor stage. Ron had the inner tube of a bicycle wheel in his left hand. He stood silently on the stage watching the children as they chattered away. A few of the boys were wrestling behind the stage, there were animated conversations, flirtations, lots of restless activity. After a few minutes, several of the youngsters turned to Ron and asked him what he was doing with the inner tube. He didn't say a word but gestured to the students to come up and sit on the stage. He arranged them in a circle, still without saying a word, and then put the inner tube in the center of the circle. As he was doing this, other youngsters stopped their conversations and began to look at this silent man and his strange ritual.

Ron then gestured to the circle to pick up the inner tube. The four youngsters picked up the tube, which stretched as they leaned back. Then Ron pointed at other students and indicated that they should come up to the stage, sit in particular spots, and take hold of the tube too. Ron's selections were not random. He had been observing the youngsters for several days and knew which cliques existed, knew the bullies, the victims, the loners, and the leaders. His educational goal (as is his goal in life) was to develop cooperation in the group. He sat enemies next to each other, merged cliques, joined loners together, put leaders next to bullies. It was beautifully orchestrated; Ron had a clear idea of where he hoped our group could go, and unobtrusively, with the sensibility of an experienced teacher, he focused everyone's attention on the collective task of stretching the inner tube to make a larger and larger circle. After the tube was stretched to ten times its original size and the circle had expanded to include most of the students, Ron suggested that groups of three students alternately sit and stand while still holding the inner tube. With his help, rhythms were set up as groups of students rose and fell with the tube. Then they bunched together and slowly moved apart, stretching the tube to what seemed the limits of its strength. Ron then joined the circle, and holding his share of the tube, raised his hands over his head. Everyone followed and it seemed as if the group were pushing a rigid hoop up toward the sky. One of the students then began to lower her part of the tube to the stage floor and everyone else followed. A tube ballet came into being, with different students initiating a motion while holding the tube. Everyone was a leader and a follower. The activity ended quietly. I noticed everyone was smiling. Ron had succeeded in creating a feeling of shared fun in a group of youngsters whose customary school life is defined by competition and gossip.

He used all kinds of other common objects, such as tires, scraps of wood, styrofoam pillows, and garbage can tops, to focus the group on noncompetitive play. He got students tossing garbage can tops like discuses, seeing how many tennis balls they could stuff under their shirts, or how many of them could fit inside a truck tire. I've seen many people try similar activities using unconventional materials, yet Ron's work is qualitatively different. Most teachers pay more attention to the game and its rules or to the material used than to the children playing. I recently observed two teachers working with youngsters the same age as those at our camp. They used the same kind of materials, followed the same sequences, played the same games as Ron did, and bored the children. The impression was that they had to put the children through the game rather than be with the players, respond to the play, and change the rules if it would make for more fun. Ron has no problem with rule changes, even in midgame. He focuses on the children, not the activities or the materials (which he has control of and knows thoroughly), and responds to the flow of the game. He changes his mode from light and sweet to strenuous, depending upon the energy flow of the players. Ron won't tolerate bullying, yet loves robust fun; respects shyness and outgoingness alike and is always working to bring out his students' strengths. He seems happiest when the students don't need him, when for example he's refereeing a game and there are no fouls to call or rules to enforce. I remember him standing next to our garden, watching a particularly raucous game of kick the can. He had a wry yet gentle smile, and watched the game without once interfering with the action. He told me afterward that it was one of his most enjoyable moments at the camp. The students were playing wildly and yet within the rules, they were playing hard but not hurting each other, and most of all they were having fun and making sure by themselves that no one felt left out or inferior. In this and other games and learning situations, Ron uses his craft to mobilize his students' energies and help them to flow both more freely and more constructively. He does this without coercion or seduction and with only the subtlest manipulation. He trusts that children want to grow and knows how to create activities and structure in a group that at the same time fosters the individual expressiveness of its members and cooperation.

After the two weeks with us, Ron returned to his work at the Recreational Center for the Handicapped. About seven months later, I received a letter from Ron as well as a copy of *Shared Victory: A Collection of Unusual World Records*, a book Ron wrote and printed. Ron explained that he used our summer school as a laboratory. He was experimenting with forms of exuberance and learning how to set up contests and challenges that focused energy on shared victory. He took what he learned from our youngsters and refined and used it with the handicapped youngsters and adults he works with. The book, which is full of photos as well as Ron's text, describes contests such as the tallest inner tube sandwich, the most people standing on an inner tube, the highest inner tube climb, the tallest paper cup tower, the most tennis balls stuffed in a T-shirt, the fastest wheelchair car (wheelchairs decorated to look like sports cars), the longest inner tube hug, and the most uses of a bicycle inner tube. All these contests focus on activities that may seem silly but require skill. They lead people away from their handicaps and release energy that is often tied up in self-pity, fear, and guilt. Ron knows how to distract people from their handicaps in order to bring them closer to the sources of their own strength. His teaching sensibility, which he says has taken almost twenty years to develop, consists in part of being able to perceive in people hints of strength that most observers wouldn't notice. He can tell by a smile, by the way eyes respond to a joke or story, by the tilt of a head, or by some other indication of attention, intelligence, and humor, the strengths of the people he works with. And he relates to them in a warm, perceptive, and fair way that conveys his faith in their strength.

10.

LOVING STUDENTS
AS LEARNERS

Faith in the learner leads some teachers to find strengths where others see nothing but weakness and failure. Such faith, which is a component of teaching sensibility, is a form of what I call the love for students as learners. It is important to pause over the idea of *loving students as learners*, which is not the same as simply loving students. Each of us has only a limited amount of love we can offer, for love is not cheaply won or given. I care about all of my students, and respect them, but love grows slowly and requires attention and effort that cannot be spread around to twenty or thirty people simultaneously. Love also engages all parts of one's life, and teaching, for all its demands, is still just a part of one's total life as a parent, lover, citizen, and learner. I don't trust teachers who say they love all their students, because it isn't possible to love so many people you know so little about and will separate from in six months or a year.

Yet a certain kind of love is essential to good teaching, and that is what I choose to call loving students as learners. I once worked with a fourteen-year-old boy who could not read at all. He was very big and often defied his teachers. Occasionally he would explode with an uncontrolled and undirected violence that made people afraid to go near him. His parents came to me in despair. I promised to work with him two days a week after school. I was afraid of him too, though I considered being alone with him one of the risks and challenges of teaching. Since he had little sense of humor and seemingly no affection, I didn't particularly like him. Still, I responded to the teaching challenge, and as we worked together, loved the way he came to master first his energy, then the alphabet, and then later books and writing.

I believe the turning point in our relationship came after about a month. He had been remote during that time, politely bored with my attempts to help him read. On this day, however, he was clearly angry. I could sense an impending explosion from the way he held his thumbs tightly in his fists and looked straight down at the floor instead of at me or at the book I was trying to get him to read. After a few minutes he did explode and knocked the manuscript of a book I was working on off my desk. I exploded quicker than he did at that. Next to the people I love, my manuscripts are the most important things in my life and I told him so. I ranted on about how important writing and books were to me. He tried to pick up the manuscript, but I let him know that at that moment I couldn't trust him to do it. As I calmed down I noticed for the first time that he was afraid, almost in tears, actually trembling. I put the manuscript together and explained that books and writing were not small school things for me but central to life and understanding, that it was no joke not to be able to read, that it was a form of poverty, and that he didn't have a right to not read. I doubt that he had ever experienced an adult express so much care for learning and books—not for some relationship to a reading test or grade, but for books themselves. Anyway, his whole attitude toward reading began to change. I felt that my love of learning and my pride in teaching him gave him a very different perception of himself as a learner. For the next few weeks we talked about what was in different books. I read sections from books that dealt with subjects he was interested in, such as sea adventures and animal life. Slowly he took up phonics and simple books again, and after a while he could read. I loved to see him learning and, of course, to feel that I was some part of that process. Yet when he no longer needed my help, we parted no better friends than we began and I didn't miss our lessons, as I sometimes do. However, I took great pleasure in seeing him focus his previously undisciplined energy and learn to read. I loved him as a learner: it was a job-related affection. That affection led me to study him carefully and build on the strengths and personal interests I could tease out of him. It required that my personal feelings about him be subordinated to my feelings about him as a learner.

Teachers have preferences and can't be expected to like every student equally. And though teachers want to be liked by all their students, they shouldn't expect that to happen, either. Nevertheless, a teacher has an obligation to care about every student as a learner, just as every student should respect a decent caring teacher whether or not he or she likes that teacher.

11.

THE SUSPENSION
OF EGO
IN TEACHING

Almost every teacher is aware of being observed and judged by students. The first few years in the classroom are particularly self-conscious times, since the specter of student revolt, or of personal failure to reach students, is constantly present. Recently I had a talk with a young woman who did her student teaching with me. After two years of substitute teaching and managing to survive tending bar, driving a taxi, and doing carpentry, she finally got a full-time job teaching in a public school. After two months with her twenty-two third graders, however, she was an emotional wreck. She called me and asked for help. We met at a small restaurant. I hardly recognized her. Joan had been a confident, exuberant student teacher with an aura of gentleness and a ready kind smile. Now she looked hard-edged, jumpy, angry. When I sat down she burst into tears and confessed that she never should have tried to become a teacher, was hopeless with children, was ready to quit and go back to tending bar and being a carpenter.

I asked her what had happened in those two months. She didn't seem to know. Nothing she did with her students worked. They didn't seem to like her, which made her feel that she was either too permissive or too stern; she wanted them to like her and when she told them that, they took advantage of her. She no longer knew why they were locked up together in that room together for five hours a day.

I suggested she calm down, have a glass of wine, and try to think of her students, think of them as people with lives independent of her and school. Could she name all of them without consulting a rollbook? Could she describe each one, tell me what they could do and couldn't do?

She paused and looked troubled. It wasn't easy to make that separation. Her ego, her sense of self-esteem, of success and failure, was bound up with her relationship to the students. They weren't people separate from her sense of self at all, and this binding made it impossible to conceive of a way out of their mutual pain.

I suggested she focus on one child, call up an image of the way he or she talks, walks, or looks about the room, and then to imagine how that child feels about himself or herself. I was trying to help Joan separate her observation of children from her sense of personal involvement. It seemed to help some. She began to take a fresh approach to her class and think about their needs instead of what she expected her students to give her. She managed to remain with that class during a very stormy year and now relates to this year's class much better. By being less dependent upon and more aware of her students, Joan has become much closer to them and much more effective as a teacher.

The release from ego that the careful observation of students involves on any level of teaching makes it possible to learn their needs and strengths and consequently to help them use these strengths to meet their own needs. Recently I was approached by a neighbor whose five-year-old son is having serious problems in kindergarten. The whole system seemed to be gearing up to certify James retarded and to separate him from his friends by putting him in a special class or even an institution. James's parents are not school wise and don't know how to talk to psychologists, psychomotor experts, administrators, and teachers, all of whom seem ranged against their son. They love James and take care of him as best they can and don't want him stigmatized.

James's mother has a serious back injury and is in severe pain most of the time. His father is a logger who spends most of his time in the woods. A big, gentle man, he was a medic in Vietnam and is still struggling with visions of the horrors he lived there. He and his wife are both quiet people who communicate as much with gesture as with words, and James is similar.

When Thomas and Julie asked me to help out with James, there were two things I could do. The first was to hold the school at bay, to get the experts off James's back; the second was to take a careful look at James and develop a program for him. The first was easy, since I know the school authorities, and with a bit of persuasion they were willing to let me tutor James and leave him with his friends in kindergarten for a few months. The second was much harder. As soon as I decided to work with James, my ego became involved. I needed him to succeed as much for my sense of myself as a teacher as for him. That could lead to my putting pressure on him at the wrong time and in the wrong way, intervening before I knew enough about him to sense how he could help himself.

James was not easy to get to know. He is big for his age and as strong for a five-year-old as his logger father is for his age. James also mumbles and it is probably the combination of that and his size that first set him apart in school.

After my first visit to James's home, I wondered whether I wasn't making a mistake. Along with being barely verbal, he showed no affection, wasn't responsive, was watching me with what seemed like frightened eyes. I was apprehensive: Would I fail with him? Were the school people right?

On my second visit to James's house, I suggested we take

a walk to the grocery store, a block away. As we walked down the stairs in front of his house, a little girl called out from across the street, "James, come on, let's play."

He grunted and shook his head no. I told him there was no rush to get to the store and asked him to introduce me to his friend. We walked across the street and he said, "This is Essie."

Essie was the opposite of James—cute, verbal, and open. I asked her if she played with James a lot and she said yes and then showed me her tricycle and said James had fixed it for her.

At that point another boy, Adam, who is ten and a friend of my son Josh, passed by. I asked him if he knew James and he said yes, that James was the first person he met when he moved into town just a month ago. James had gone up to Adam's family and helped them unload their car and move in.

As James and I made our way down the block, I sensed myself watching him more closely. I also began feeling my way into his linguistic world. We walked over the cement cover of a water meter and I asked James what it was. He said, "Water feeder." We passed two girls riding tricycles. They looked away when James passed. I asked him who they were. He said, "Not friends." When I mentioned this later to Julie, she said the mother of those children wouldn't let her children play with James and that that whole family looked down on Julie and Thomas as well.

In the grocery store, James and I did a tour of the aisles. Cake mixes were "birthday cake, Julie make for me." James knew cigarettes, whiskey, wine, beer, knew what all the produce was, and asked me if I could get him a jawbreaker, "Can have candy? Goes in mouth, is hard."

I got him the jawbreaker, and as we left the store, I deliberately turned in the wrong direction. He tugged at my pants and pulled me back toward home. As we approached his house, he took the jawbreaker out of his mouth and held it up

to me, saying, "Is white, was red." He was right; the red
candy dye had dissolved and the jawbreaker turned white.

When I came home after this second time with James, my
mind was filled with the details of our walk, and with the
portrait of him that was emerging. He knew colors, could
count, made friends. In the store he showed me that he was
aware of a whole range of objects and could name or describe
them. The encounter with Adam and Essie showed a generous and curious nature, as well as mechanical ingenuity.
James clearly had made a place for himself in his small world
despite clear hostility as indicated by the other two girls we
encountered on our walk. James had many strengths and that
was what I was looking for. What he didn't know was not
relevant; one has to find strengths first and then help the
learner use these strengths to nurture growth.

During that walk I had to suspend my ego in order to
understand how others saw James and perceive his particular
ways of relating to things and people. Had I let my ego get in
the way, my desire to succeed with James might have caused
me to take the initiative and begin teaching and making demands upon him prematurely. I had to see and feel who he
was before developing a program to foster his growth.

After the walk, I had specifics to work with and saw a
lovely part of him that never had surfaced in school. I also
began to understand his language. He especially loved to talk
about his father ("my Thomas" he called him) and showed me
his father's baseball glove just before I left his house. On my
way home I remembered seeing James wandering around
during the men's softball games that took place every Sunday,
in which his father was one of the best hitters in the league.
James would grab a bat and imitate Thomas's swing whenever
he could. Some people laughed at him at the games and called
him retarded. But no kindergartner I'd ever seen could swing
a bat or hit a ball as he could.

James's energy was clearly tied up in baseball and

Thomas. With Thomas's help, a simple softball-oriented curriculum could get him through everything expected in kindergarten. The colors of uniforms, the scoring of runs, the names and locations of teams, the standings in the league, and the shapes of bats, balls, and bases just about covered all the concepts and ideas in James's teachers' rigid kindergarten curriculum. I got a copy of the curriculum, translated it into softball terms. I made two sets of flash cards. One set had pictures of a bat, a ball, a glove, a pitcher, a catcher, and an umpire, and the other set had the words *bat, ball, pitcher, catcher,* and *umpire.* I asked Julie and Thomas to show the cards to James every night and to match the words with the pictures. I also wrote down the names of all of the teams in Thomas's softball league and colored them in with their team colors. James already knew the team colors and I used them to help him learn about letters and sounds. Finally Thomas and I designed a softball board game for James in which he kept score as well as played. It was a way to get him to learn to recognize numbers, count and do simple arithmetic.

I believe that if I had not been able to suspend my desire to jump right in and start teaching James the minute we met, not been able to watch him without intervening, his energy sources would have remained hidden and no program I developed, however sophisticated, would have been as effective as the softball focus.

I remember a different context in which the suspension of ego enabled me to turn a potentially chaotic situation into a pleasant learning experience. I was substitute teaching for a friend who had to take care of a family crisis. I was called at eight in the morning and arrived at school at eight forty-five. The students had been in the room since eight-thirty and had managed to organize several games, dismantle a bookcase, turn over chairs and a large table. I knew my friend was having trouble with the class and intuited that his absence had released even more chaos. When I arrived, the door was open and I stood watching what was going on. It was clear that I'd have to step in and act in order to get through the day. Where to begin, though? How to step in and convert the disorder to some form of positive activity? I looked for details that would indicate who the class leaders were, listened to get a sense of the language the children used with each other, watched for clusters of children to estimate how many different things were happening simultaneously. I had to suspend my ego, and not jump in too soon or worry about whether I would be liked or successful, but rather gather as much information about the class as I could, as quickly as possible.

The largest group of students was playing around with a basketball, shooting it toward the teacher's desk, bouncing it off the ceiling, passing it wildly around the room. I decided that taming the basketball game would refocus the class's energy and establish enough structure so that I would be able to talk to the whole group and plan a full day together with them. I waited for a downcourt pass that was coming my way and stepped inside the room and caught the pass. Everyone froze for a moment—who was this stranger with their basketball?

I told the group that I was going to be their teacher for a day and turned to a boy whom I perceived to be a leader and asked, "Does your teacher always let you play basketball in the room?"

He said, "Yes."

I knew he was jiving me and I could have pretended to be angry and sat everyone down and proceeded with a lecture on classroom decorum. But lectures like that are no fun to give and don't produce results unless they are backed up by coercive force, which I had no intention of using. Better to go with the energy of the basketball game and use it as a positive focus. My response was:

"Where's the basket?"

He looked at me as if I were crazy.

"A basketball game has a basket and rules. If you play in here all the time, I wouldn't want to change anything. Where's the basket?"

One of the students caught on that I was willing to play along and let everyone save face rather than punish them, and she brought me the wastebasket. I accepted that as the basket, drew a scorecard on the chalkboard and a foul line on the classroom floor and set up a foul-shooting contest. Ten shots for everyone from the foul line to the wastebasket. Three scorekeepers at the chalkboard, two students retrieving the ball, two holding the basket, the rest on line waiting to shoot, unless they wanted to read a book or play a quiet game somewhere else in the room. Those were the first activities for the day. The next was to talk about what usually went on in the classroom and plan a day together. My goal was to shift the focus of group energy away from taking advantage of their teacher's absence to helping me contrive to find a pleasant way to pass the day together. It would have been impossible if I responded by taking charge right away and laying down the law because my ego as a teacher was threatened.

Children pick up on their teachers' weaknesses and sometimes use them to shatter classroom authority. They can make fun of your clothes or breath or nose or walk or voice. In my case, students seem to pick on my flyaway hair, as one youngster called it. When I first began teaching, I wasted energy worrying about whether to cut my hair or defend myself against some student's snide remarks. That energy would more profitably have been invested in making the content of my teaching more interesting. After a while I learned how to make casual fun of my own hair and move on to more important things.

Another way students had of undermining my confidence was to make fun of lessons I had meticulously prepared. For example, during my second year of teaching, the theme of the fifth-grade social studies curriculum was the Industrial Revolution. I had spent the summer studying ways of building a working model of an early factory. I built or bought miniature models of factory tools and connected them through a series of belts and pulleys to a small steam engine. My idea was to demonstrate a simple version of a working factory to my class and then build a large, fairly accurate scale model of a cotton mill while studying the psychological, social, and economic effects of industrialization. Sometime during the first week of school I brought in the steam engine and a simple piston press that was powered by the engine. I was proud of my teaching plans and sure my students would be excited by them. One of the students filled the engine with water and another lit the can of Sterno under the boiler. As the water began to heat, we could hear sputtering and rumbling inside the engine, and a bit of steam escaped through the safety valve. Suddenly a voice from the back of the room proclaimed, "It's farting," and everybody started laughing and holding their noses. I was shattered, my face became red; my wonderful ideas had been turned into nothing but a silly joke. I blew out the fire, put the engine away, and insisted that everyone get out their workbooks and do an extra assignment. It took me several days to recover enough confidence to do something interesting again and try to get my students out of the workbooks that I used as a punishment.

If a similar thing happened to me these days, I'd laugh with my students at the farting engine and show them how the force created by such a blow-off could be used to run a machine. I would go with their energy and refocus it on learning, without destroying the good feeling created by sharing a joke.

I remember another instance where a similar twist on a planned lesson occurred. It happened a few years ago, after I'd had over fifteen years of teaching experience and learned how to control my ego and laugh with my students. I was teaching a combined kindergarten and first-grade class and had prepared a week's worth of explorations of the phenomena of light. The subject was introduced by giving each child a small mirror and some three-by-five cards that had capital letters written on them. My intention was to introduce the notion of symmetry and have the class discover which letters were symmetrical and which weren't, using the mirrors. As I explained the meaning of symmetry to the class and demonstrated it with a larger mirror and some drawings I'd prepared, there was a slight commotion in one corner of the room. I ignored it for a few minutes and went on. It got louder and as I turned to say something I found myself blinded. Four students had discovered how to use their mirrors to reflect sunlight into peoples' eyes and found that much more interesting and challenging than learning what symmetry was.

I went with the energy released by the students' discovery and reflected the sun back at them, using my mirror. Then I suggested we all try to focus the sunlight we captured on one spot on the ceiling. After managing that, one student suggested we have sunspot races and before long there were reflected spots of sunlight racing around the room, chasing each other. I joined in the games and at the same time reformulated my teaching plans. We'd start with reflections and angles, maybe move to shadows, and eventually find our way back to symmetry. Actually it didn't much matter to me how (or even whether) we got to symmetry. What was much more important was experimenting with the nature of light and trying to devote energy to understanding that phenomenon. The homework assignment for that day was to draw a picture explaining how someone managed to blind me. The picture had to show the sun, the mirror, me, and the path of light from the sun to my eyes.

12.

THE TEACHER
AS TRICKSTER

It takes experience to learn how to take a joke, to reformulate a lesson, and to perceive the sources of student energy. And no matter how much experience you've had or how finely developed your teaching sensibility becomes, you'll always be tested, confounded, and challenged. One of the beauties of teaching is that there is no limit to one's growth as a teacher, just as there is no knowing beforehand how much your students can learn. I was recently reminded of this when I tried to work with Joyce, a fifteen-year-old I encountered in a juvenile prison. Her teacher, who is a friend of mine, asked me to spend some time with her. She was the most confounding youngster he or any of the staff had ever encountered. She had a severely retarded younger sister and was a master at acting as if she were retarded. Everyone knew she wasn't. There were flashes of brilliance in class, references she occasionally made to books and newspaper articles that belied retardation. However, the strongest proof of her intelligence was that she was her cottage's lawyer, the leader and representative of the other girls who lived with her.

But the first time I saw Joyce, I could have sworn she was retarded. Her mouth drooped, she slouched down in her chair and hung her hands limply down almost to the floor. There were about a dozen other youngsters in the room and I talked to them when she refused to acknowledge my existence. Every few minutes I looked straight at her, hoping to engage her eyes at least once. I was talking about redwood trees (the prison was in Appalachia, and none of the students had heard of the redwoods that are still hanging on in my part of California). I was trying to explain that redwoods never really die unless they're pulled out by the stump, that new shoots come off the root system when a first growth tree is falled, as the loggers say, and that second-growth trees grow up out of the roots and form a ring around the old stump. I mentioned that the ring is called a widow's ring or fairies' ring, and happened to glance toward Joyce. Her eyes were alert, her body leaned forward. She was attentive, alive until our eyes engaged, and then she returned to her comatose retarded stance.

If I were a psychologist I would design therapeutic strategies to discover the cause of her behavior and undo her past hurts. But I'm a teacher, not a psychologist, and concerned with present and future growth, not with unearthing and undoing the damage that took place in my student's past. I had to give Joyce a way to use her strengths to acquire specific skills as well as a love of learning in the present. The past, the personal and social hurts she felt, had to be acknowledged but then discarded as irrelevant to my teaching task, which was to help her develop skills, confidence, and thoughtfulness that might be useful in her difficult life.

A teacher can't be everything—parent, psychologist, social worker, friend, lover, constant companion. One of the hardest things to learn as a young teacher is what it is that one can be *as* teacher. Simply put, a teacher can provide a pathway to new skills, information, perceptions, and personal strengths; can provide young people with a knowledge of how to learn and to teach themselves, no matter what the circumstances of life have forced upon them. A teacher's role is to strengthen young people, to build sensitivity and intelligence, and to refuse to make any final judgment on what it is possible for any young person to do—which brings me back to Joyce's eyes.

Joyce wanted to listen but didn't want it to be known that she could hear or understand. Therefore her intelligence, as her life, would remain fugitive unless there was a way for her to drop her cover. Appearing retarded protected her, since many people accepted her act and left her alone or excused her for doing things that were illegal since "she didn't know any better." Nevertheless, Joyce was in prison and was headed toward permanent confinement in a home for the retarded. Her retarded act worked in small ways but led to a loss of self and spiritual death. What could a teacher do in this situation, what modest but possibly important role could a teacher play in this young person's life? Of course, this question, raised so abstractly and morally, faces teachers, faced me with Joyce, in a different form: What can I do now to help this person before me, given what I understand about her resistance to learning and fear of growth.

With Joyce, I saw no route for myself but what could be called the trickster's way. Knowing how to trick students who believe they are stupid and incapable of learning into allowing their intelligence and imagination to develop is another part of teaching sensibility. I would only be with Joyce for a week, would probably never see her again. I needed to get her off guard, to let her see that she didn't need to use the mask of retardation to survive and that her alert mind could be a more powerful weapon than her dull eyes. It was also essential that she be helped to open up to the teachers at the prison who cared about her.

There were several things that were clear in developing a learning strategy for Joyce:

First, she could not be unmasked. It was possible to trick her into showing her awareness and intelligence in front of other teachers and staff, but it wouldn't help Joyce. Most likely she'd assume another, more hostile role. She had to decide to come out herself, in ways that she was comfortable with.

Second, she had to understand my intention—that is, she had to understand me as teacher and not as judge. Somehow she had to feel that her success was my success and her failure my failure. Most students in our foolishly competitive schools feel that they are in a battle with their teachers and that when students fail teachers succeed, and when students succeed they do it despite their teachers. Teaching well implies the opposite—our only success lies in how well our pupils do.

Third, Joyce would have to laugh at how I brought her out. As the hustlers I grew up with in New York used to say, cool the mark out. Joyce was the mark, the person involved in my educational trick, and she had to be cooled out, to think that the trick was interesting enough to make a good story and not embarrass her for being taken. The difference between my hustling and that of most street hustlers is that I was doing it for Joyce, not against her.

Given these three conditions, I spent the first two days worrying about what to do. It never comes easy, and sometimes one simply can't reach some youngsters, no matter how much one wants to. But with Joyce I was lucky. I walked into the library one day after lunch and Joyce was the only one there. She was lost in some paperback romance and didn't notice me. As soon as she saw me her eyes drooped, she closed the book, and pretended she was just admiring the picture on the cover. I asked her if she was interested in knowing what the book told about the people on the cover. She nodded dumbly and I made up the most preposterous story about unrequited love in nineteenth-century Russia. After a few minutes of hearing my foolish tale she couldn't restrain herself and corrected me, placing the book in Alabama after the Civil War and naming several of the main characters. Then she caught herself, tried to put on the mask, but realized she'd been caught too far from it and laughed with me. I promised her not to tell anybody, but insisted she listen for several minutes. I told her which teachers cared for her, talked of the intelligence I saw in her eyes, and concluded, as the librarian was returning from lunch, that she was fooling herself if she believed her pretense would get her out of prison and on in life; what it would give her was the security of lifelong institutionalization, if that was what she wanted.

I saw Joyce only once after that, in a small group where she was talking freely and intelligently. Since then, as my friend at the prison has told me, Joyce has come out selectively and cautiously. She uses the mask occasionally, but is willing to read and talk and participate fully in classes where she trusts the teacher. Whether this means Joyce's life will have more hope isn't clear—the world is cruel to young women with prison records and a reputation for being retarded. Still, as teachers, my friend and I did something other than moan about her past and complain about how she couldn't learn. We tried to do what all serious teachers I've known try to do—assume that every student can learn and become strong, sensitive, and intelligent, no matter what hurts or deprivations they bring to us.

13.

PROBLEM KIDS

OR

PROBLEM CLASSROOMS?

Joyce was not an easy person to work with. Imagine a class of twenty or more students with several Joyces in it. Most teachers have classes of more than twenty students to work with and care about. When one or two children require the attention Joyce did, it can seem like an unfair and even impossible burden. The temptation to push problem children off on specialists such as psychologists, counselors, and special education teachers becomes enormous. The aura of specialist implies that exclusion will benefit the child and make the regular classroom teacher's life easier. But it usually doesn't work that way. If a classroom is full of tension or boredom, referral out of it, no matter how stigmatizing, can be a welcome relief. Also, once one youngster leaves and is offered more freedom and personal attention in a special program, getting referred out of the classroom becomes a matter of prestige for the others. I've seen classrooms where "problem students" emerge in a very regular way. As soon as one student is referred out, another takes his or her place, almost to the point of imitating the behavior that produced the referral. In one district I observed, several classes were reduced to ten or eleven students by such referrals, without anyone ever asking why this absurd defection was occurring.

I remember a similar phenomenon that took place in

Berkeley about fifteen years ago. At that time there were many students who were bored in the high school and un- afraid to defy school authority. They were also straight-A stu- dents who didn't qualify to attend the district continuation school, which had a concentration of highly motivated teach- ers and an interesting curriculum. Several of the students decided to get into the continuation school despite restric- tions that limited the school to students who were discipline problems or were failing at the high school. They went to their principal and asked for a transfer, which was predictably refused. As planned, they left the principal's office, picked up a carton of spray paints they had stored in the bushes, and proceeded to decorate the school with elaborately cal- ligraphed multicolored graffiti. In two days they were all in the continuation school.

One or two difficult youngsters or especially a half dozen are often symptomatic of a deeper, wider, but suppressed student opposition. Certainly some students bring problems from the streets or the home into their classroom, but in my experience the strength of peer pressure is so great that in a congenial learning environment the other students keep the unhappy fringe under control. When there are students like Joyce or like the Berkeley Five, as they called themselves, the first question to ask is whether the students' resistance to learning is justified. The next step is to discover a way to reach out to the resistant or defiant students and take their pain, their objections, their suggestions, and their defiance seriously.

It's easy to give up on extremely difficult youngsters. I remember Allan, one of my high school students, and Martin, a first grader I had in my class several years later. They were remarkably similar, though one was sixteen and the other was six. Allan and Martin had to be watched at every moment. If another student came too close to them, they would explode into a violent rage that could be dangerous. Neither had any friends or discernible interests and they both went around grumbling about how terrible the world was. They took up an inordinate amount of my time and energy. I always had them in the corner of my eye when I was working with other students. I spent individual time with them before, after, and during class, restrained them when they exploded, steered them toward other students who I intuited would be natural friends for them. During the first year we spent together, the only sign of change was a decrease in the frequency of explosions and a willingness to reveal one interest, theater for Allan and fast and loud motorcycles for Martin.

Refusing to give up on either of them (Martin, I knew, would be suspended forthwith by the teacher he would be assigned to for the next semester), I kept them for a second year, though not without wondering whether their presence would be damaging to my new students.

They completely surprised me when they returned to school in September. Both Allan and Martin were kind and welcoming to the new students. They knew me and knew how the classroom functioned, and they were older than the other youngsters. As Allan explained, it was the first time he knew more than the other children and was in control. My investment in another year with them paid off, but not in ways that I'd anticipated. They took advantage of their seniority and that undid their isolation.

Not every isolated child, of course, is violent. One encounters shy, lonely children who are obedient, work hard, and yet are as remote from group life as Allan or Martin. I remember Cindee, a girl in a sixth-grade class I taught in New York City. She never talked in class, never volunteered, froze up when called on to participate in a discussion, and came and left school alone. Her written work was excellent and had a spark of wildness that wasn't apparent in her behavior. She loved to describe people metaphorically, as empty coffee cups, cracked whiskey glasses, ripped nylons, stunted sunflowers. Occasionally one of her characters was described positively. I remember an energetic aunt she described as a "glowing stove, a bubbling kettle and a one carat diamond ring."

Cindee's writing set me to teaching the whole class about metaphor, both for their benefit and as a strategy to bring Cindee into the group. If she got excited enough about the subject, she just might forget her shyness and share some of her wonderful linguistic imagination with us.

I tried several simple exercises. One was having students make increasingly complicated similes. We started with the form:

she was as _____ as a _____

and then got increasingly complex

she was as _____ as a _____ (who)/(that) _____
she was as _____ as a _____   _____
     (who)/(that) _____

A typical response was:

She was as red as a beet.
She was as red as a beet that was rotting.
She was as red as a white beet that was rotting.

My guess about Cindee's interest in the exercise was correct. Her mind started working quickly; she couldn't keep quiet and shared at least half a dozen of her creations with us, one of which was:

He was as calm as a hurricane.
He was as calm as a hurricane that got stronger as it came up the coast from Florida.
He was as calm as a purple hurricane that got stronger as it came up the coast from Florida.

Cindee explained to us that she had come up the coast from the Miami area to settle in New York, and experienced a lot of hurricanes when she was young. She didn't like the women's names they gave the hurricanes, so she gave them colors.

Within a few weeks of her first excited opening up, Cindee became a valuable and frequent participant in our discussions. And slowly, because she began to sense the respect of other students, she moved toward them and began to make friends.

In this case my strategy worked. If it hadn't, it was important to wait for another opportunity. Teachers have to be patient and at the same time jump in if they see an occasion to help one of their students. It is essential to assume that children want to be part of the group, and that isolation is painful. Time spent trying to help someone who doesn't fit into a group is also time spent understanding the group itself. The more I teach, the more convinced I am that one of the essential roles of the teacher is to make it possible for even the most difficult and unhappy individuals to feel supported and welcome within a group of their peers. It frees them to learn and to share what they know in return for the welcome they receive. The difficult ones, once integrated into a group, provide the strength and spirit to the whole that for me as a teacher results in a challenging and yet congenial class.

PART III

THE CONTENT OF LEARNING

14.

CONTENT

AND CONTROL

Recently I overheard a conversation between my children and some visiting friends of theirs, comparing their high schools and talking about teachers they loved and hated. One girl spoke of a teacher she had had whom she couldn't decide whether to love or to hate. She liked him because he was kind and respectful to all the students. Yet he never taught anything and let students do whatever they wanted, so long as they caused no trouble. She had spent a year in his math class listening to tapes of her favorite records and pretending to do math, and a year in his English class filling up pages in her private diary. Now, several years later, she was suffering from having missed a year of math and had trouble writing simple essays.

This teacher sounded as if he had developed a decent teaching sensibility without having much interest in teaching anything. Teaching does not consist solely of making youngsters feel good about themselves. It involves helping students acquire understanding, knowledge, and skills they didn't previously have. To do this, it is essential to enable students to feel good about themselves as learners and to create an atmosphere that enables them to focus energy on learning. But this is not all there is to teaching well. Thought has to be given to the content of what is to be learned and to the way this content is to be presented.

Another way of avoiding teaching is by relying exclusively on a textbook, workbooks, and other commercially packaged learning materials. Teaching is reduced to administering a set curriculum without giving any thought to the substance of what the students are learning or to their particular needs. Learning to teach well consists in part of finding ways of avoiding these extremes, of dealing with content as well as feeling and relating what is to be learned to the interests, skills, and strengths of the learners. It is not easy to maintain this balance, even after years of teaching.

The first few months I taught a combined kindergarten–first grade, I swung from an obsession with understanding my students to an obsession with the content of what I was teaching. Five- and six-year-olds in a classroom were a mystery to me, even though one of my own children was six and another almost five. I didn't understand how to deal with the needs and demands of twenty-nine of them, nor did I have a firm intuition about how much they could learn and how they went about dealing with new material. I'd already been teaching young people aged eleven to seventeen for about twelve years, but these little ones were new to me and I was anxious. How could I fill up five hours in a useful and not chaotic manner? I tried to walk myself through the first day in my imagination, but never managed to get much past ten-thirty in the morning. There was too much to worry about, as there always is for a new teacher or even an experienced teacher going into a completely new situation. There are twenty-nine strangers to meet and get to know and understand. There is subject matter to structure and present. There is time to fill up. There are details to deal with—late and absence notes, attendance forms, missing lunches, lost coats, sweaters, and hats. Being new to a situation that makes so many simultaneous demands invariably implies letting some things go while mastering others, and the sensibility/content tension emerges very strongly. Should you concentrate on discovering who the students are and how their energy can be focused and lean on workbooks and mechanical exercises for a while, or would it be better to concentrate on interesting content well presented and be a strict disciplinarian until you and your students get to know each other better? I've never been able to decide which strategy to use, and I go back and forth for a few months until feeling and content come together. In a new teaching situation, I do, however, always begin in a more structured way than I will come to. It is easier to loosen up than to tighten up. Relaxing rules and structures is seen as an act of trust and affection, tightening up as a punishment if not a covert declaration of war.

I decided to teach kindergarten and first grade as part of a teacher training program that Cynthia Brown and I set up at The Center for Open Learning and Teaching in Berkeley. During the first year of our program, I taught classes on curriculum development, the teaching of writing and mathematics, and games in the classroom. After that year, one of our graduates suggested that my work would be more effective if I was in the classroom with children full time and used the classroom as one of the model learning environments for our program. I agreed. Most of our students wanted to be kindergarten through third-grade teachers, so I decided to take a chance on being able to provide a model even though kindergarten and first grade was foreign territory to me.

I spent the week before school began arranging the classroom. I decided to structure it somewhat like the room where I did my own writing. I'm usually working on a half-dozen or more writing projects at a time and each project has to have its own location in my study. Some projects are half completed and others in various stages of revision. A few are just being researched. Each one needs a space appropriate to its stage of development and also needs to be easily accessible. I saw a relationship between the projects I was personally involved in and those I hoped would engage my students. I wanted to emphasize process and hoped that many different activities in different stages of completion would eventually be going on simultaneously. For that reason, I organized the classroom around six learning centers. Each center occupied its own space and had a different focus. One had to do with counting, measuring, and other mathematical ideas. A second was science oriented and was organized around the theme of magnetism. The third center was a playhouse renamed The Haunted House in the hope that boys as well as girls would play there. In addition, there was an art center and a block-building center, where the children could even build live-in block structures if they cared to. The sixth was a literacy center, focused on reading and writing. It consisted of several bookcases of picture and easy-reading books, a table with rubber stamps, staplers, stencils, paper, crayons, and other enticements to writing, as well as a long table with room for eight students. I intended to sit at that table and work with students on reading and writing while keeping an eye on the other activities in the room.

In each of the centers I hung a board with five hooks on it. There was a peg containing thirty rings mounted near the classroom door. My idea was to let the children choose, several times a day, a center they wanted to be in and to give each child a ring to hang on a hook in the center they chose. Once the five hooks were filled up, no one else could use the center for that period. I structured it that way not for any deep educational reason, but because I was nervous about controlling the children. My fears were that everyone would want to play with the blocks or be in The Haunted House, that fights would develop over the magnets or the scale in the math center—most of all, that I would end up that first day a powerless adult surrounded by twenty-nine wild five- and six-year-olds.

The plan for six learning centers didn't last a week. The system was clumsy and the children didn't want to group themselves into fives. The first morning, several rings were lost, and by the end of the first day, the board with five hooks that was hanging in the math center had somehow migrated to The Haunted House, where it had become the control panel of a spaceship. To my surprise, the reading center was the most popular attraction for the first week. Most of my students had already been told that the main reason for going to school was to learn to read. They wanted "real" school, not play school. Almost all of them had attended child care centers or been part of Head Start and early learning centers. They had graduated into kindergarten and expected more than play.

Also, they didn't want to go to different centers. They wanted to go to the place where something interesting was happening. If I began to read a story, most of the children would wander or sneak over to the reading center to hear it. If a parent came in with a special science or art project, almost everyone wanted to be part of it. Otherwise the science as well as the math center was a disaster. There just wasn't enough material in each of them to keep the children interested without adult supervision. After two weeks, I merged the math and science centers and added strategy games such as chess, checkers, and Wari, an African strategy game. I also spent time during lunch and yard break teaching several children how to play the games, encouraging them to teach the rest of the class. The block center was beginning to have its regular devotees, and three or four of the boys would have done nothing else if I hadn't required them to read with me once a day and to participate in the two study sessions I added to the plan. That was the main departure from my original plan, a response to the need to present the whole class with enough content on which to focus the rest of the activities.

15.

THEMATIC TEACHING

Of the two study sessions I added to the curriculum of the kindergarten–first grade I taught in the Berkeley Center for Open Learning and Teaching, one was devoted to reading, writing, literature, theater, or some form of group language activity. I read stories and discussed them with the class, or had children read, tell, or act out stories. We wrote collective stories and generally used that period to help students focus on language activities they could pursue either individually or in groups at other times during the day. My goal was to talk with my students about the content of stories, to discuss the way a piece of writing emerges, and to transfer to them some of the excitement I feel about reading and writing books. There was no testing or grading. Even the students who didn't actively participate in discussions were listening and thinking. This came out when I sat down to read individually with each of the children (which I did at least three times a week) and they chatted about our group discussions.

The other group session (which usually lasted about twenty minutes) was devoted to science, social studies, or math. I knew from previous teaching experience that one way to tie our activities together was to introduce a theme that could be examined for a week or two through science, math, the arts, reading, and writing. The theme would then be worked into the activities in the centers and give the whole class day or week some unity.

Some of the themes we explored were sound, light, machines, buildings, measuring, counting, flying, living in East Africa and West Africa, and water. Preparing to focus on a theme for a week or two takes a lot of work, especially the first time you try to teach it. The theme has to be explored from different points of view and specific activities planned that are likely to interest and be comprehensible to your students. For example, the theme "sound" can be treated:

- through science by considering vibrations, animals' sounds, or the human voice
- through math by considering frequencies on a radio dial, a guitar, a piano, and a stretched rubber band
- through art by making musical instruments or singing
- through fantasy by creating scary sounds and other sound effects
- through reading and writing by studying different musical or language notation systems

My strategy with the theme of sound was to translate concepts, information, and experiments I had researched into activities that five- and six-year-olds could participate in. Luckily I overprepared and gathered more material on sound than could be dealt with in a two-week unit, for some of my favorite experiments were flops. Others, which bored me, turned out to be exceptionally rich stimulants to learning. For example, I made a large frame and stretched rubber bands over it. It was easy to hold down the rubber bands at different points and simulate musical scales. After one or two twangs, however, the children were only interested in shooting the rubber bands around the room. On the other hand, blowing into bottles to produce sounds led to the mastery of sophisticated ideas. Initially I was opposed to the idea of making bottle whistles. Connie, my student teacher, suggested it and

I wisely trusted her instinct. She brought cartons of empty wine, beer, and pop bottles to class and each student picked out a bottle. They experimented with blowing into them. Connie then suggested that the students arrange themselves according to the bottles that made similar sounds. Soon we had a bass section, a high-pitched soprano section, and a miscellaneous middle. An orchestra was formed and the class composed several simple songs in three parts. At that point, one of the girls asked Connie and me how the bottles made sounds. I asked what she meant and she clarified her question by saying she didn't think the bottle was doing anything to make a sound, and if you just blew out your breath into the air a sound wasn't made, so she wanted to know where the sound came from.

Fortunately some of the students remembered from the rubber band fiasco that the sounds made by the bands were caused by their vibrating. They also had watched the strings on our piano and the head on a drum vibrate when hit. I had been using the word "vibrate" frequently and one of the boys concluded that something must be vibrating to make the bottle sounds, only he couldn't understand what it could be.

The girl who had asked the original question suddenly jumped up, shouting, "I got it, I got it." She couldn't contain the pleasure she felt discovering that, as she put it, "It's the air inside—you can't even see it, but it's vibrating." It was one of those wonderful moments of discovery that make teaching so fulfilling. All the children turned to their bottles and blew into them, softly at first and then with as much breath as they could command. Several children burst out laughing. It seemed very funny to them that air hitting the insides of a bottle could make so many different kinds of sounds.

The strength of this insight and the energy it released allowed me to take the subject of sound much farther than I'd intended. We sorted the bottles into sizes and matched the size of a bottle with the pitch it made, developed some approximate scales, created some musical compositions, and even invented a notation to transcribe the music.

The next year, when I again introduced the theme of sound, I used the bottles but their effect wasn't as magical. They still provided insight into the nature of sound and were useful, but what excited that second class was a recording of the underwater sounds of a whale. Sound traveling through water over thousands of miles caused them to pause and think about the nature of sound just as vibrating air in a bottle had done for the previous class. The concepts both groups managed to arrive at were the same, though their way to them was completely different.

Thematic teaching provides a wonderful opportunity to approach interesting content from many different perspectives. It also illustrates one of the most important guides to effective teaching: that there are many different routes to acquiring understanding and a teacher has to master as many of them as possible. A major teaching error is to assume that because a student doesn't grasp a particular explanation, experiment, or lesson, he or she can't function on its level of complexity. Not getting across should be a challenge to teach differently, and not an occasion to label a student.

Recently I've been teaching computer programming. In order to be able to write interesting programs in a particular computer language, such as PILOT, BASIC, or Pascal, it is essential to understand the fundamental structure of that language. It is not a matter of memorizing a vocabulary list and using it mechanically so much as understanding the flow involved in a program. This consists of seeing the relationship of different parts of the program to each other and to the idea you are trying to program. Some students can acquire this understanding by following a textbook. Others simply do not seem to be able to move from the printed page to the dynamic screen and the functioning program. These students are not incapable of programming. In fact, they come to understand computer language by drawing diagrams, or by running a given program thirty or forty times and analyzing it, or even by setting a programming problem for themselves and then acquiring the program language in the bits and pieces they need to solve their problem. None of these approaches produces any better programmers than the others, and each of them if used exclusively might lead some students to give up on even trying to understand computing.

It should be a basic teaching maxim that if an explanation fails with a particular student, another tack should be taken. Too many teachers deal with students who do not understand by repeating the same explanations until both students and teachers give up.

16.

MASTERY

OF CONTENT

Being able to approach whatever one is teaching from different directions requires one to think about and master the content, even (and sometimes especially) in the teaching of kindergarten and first-grade students. For example, one of the most important things for first graders to understand is the relationship between spoken language and written language. Many, possibly most, children grasp quite easily the relationship of letters to sounds and groupings of letters to words and sentences. But some need to be helped to understand how reading and writing relate to stories and speech. The most natural way to illustrate this is to draw a letter and make a sound and keep on doing that until the child gets the relationship. If that doesn't work, repetition becomes a source of frustration and confusion.

There are other approaches, though. It's possible to begin with a word instead of a letter and gradually build up a repertoire of words a child recognizes before leaping to the sound-symbol equivalence. It's also possible to explain that relationship by analogy. There are many people who think more effectively through analogy than through direct description. I remember trying to get my student John to understand a few simple letter-sound equivalents for several weeks, and just about giving up. I noticed that he liked to play around at the piano and pretended to understand musical notation the way a lot of three- and four-year-olds pretend to understand writing. One afternoon I joined him at the keyboard and asked what the music on the piano stand said. John played several keys and told me that it said for him to play those notes. Then I drew a staff and a middle C and played that note. He did the same thing and we took turns writing and playing notes. When he seemed to be getting a bit bored, I told him that letters did the same thing for speaking that written notes did for music. He didn't seem to understand what I meant. However, the next day he brought me a book and asked if the voice was like a piano and talking like playing music. I said yes and showed him how the letter *m* told you to say "Mmm" and the letter *p* to say the sound "p." We developed the correlations of letters to sounds for several weeks, by which time he was reading with about the same competency as the students who got the sound-symbol connection right away. It's important for teachers to remember that early learning isn't better learning, and that once you have mastered a skill it doesn't much matter how you got there.

Another tactic I've occasionally used to reach someone who is having trouble understanding a concept consists of stating something that is clearly not true, silly, or absurd in order to illuminate it. I remember working with Raymond, an eight-and-a-half-year-old boy who couldn't read. I sat down with him and read a simple story, making sure that not one letter was sounded correctly. If a sentence said, "Here is Sam," I'd read it, "Wopn mr Rif," or some such nonsense. By the second page, he began to look at me as if I were crazy. After listening awhile, he said, "That book doesn't say that!" I asked him what it did say and his response was that it told a story. I replied that books couldn't talk and therefore they couldn't tell stories. He saw the point that books tell stories with letters and that therefore letters weren't just some arbitrary marks that teachers insisted he learn. Of course, the insight didn't create instant reading skills. There is no such magical event. What it did was help him to guide himself to mastery of letters, words, and ultimately stories over the next few months.

There are many other modes of explanation, such as drawing diagrams, providing examples, or even improvising a dramatic presentation of an idea. All of these techniques require a mastery of the content you are teaching so that you are free to play with it.

I've mentioned this need for mastery of content to a number of teachers and some of them replied that it's impossible for them to know everything about the subjects they teach. Of course they're right, but mastery of a subject does not consist of knowing everything about it.

The question of how much knowledge elementary and secondary school teachers should have is not an easy one to answer. Consider an elementary school teacher who works with five- and six-year-olds and another who works with eleven- and twelve-year-olds. How much should they know about reading, writing, and arithmetic? Should they both know the same things? Should the one who works with younger children know the arithmetic taught to older ones and how it can be taught? Should the teacher of the older students know anything about the teaching of beginning readers and the presentation of concepts such as counting and number? Should both teachers be expected to know high school algebra and English? These may sound like facetious questions, yet I know many primary teachers who could not pass high school competency tests today, even though they once had to, and who claim they need to know little more than do the students they teach. In fact, one of the most infuriating situations in many public schools is the resistance of teachers of grades four and above to learning how to teach beginning reading and math. They would rather fail students who come to them not knowing how to read than figure out ways of teaching beginning reading to older children.

I believe that all elementary and secondary school teachers should be at ease with almost everything taught in elementary and secondary school. There are some exceptions. All teachers can't master the languages and advanced math and science taught in our better high schools. But they should have a command of what we normally expect young people to know by graduation and be able to apply that knowledge. They should also know about teaching techniques and strategies at all grade levels so they can mix and match technique and content to fit the needs and styles of their students. This holds for private as well as public school teachers.

Every class of children is unique and therefore curriculum must be shaped and formed to meet the needs and styles of each new class. There is no way of knowing what children can't learn. That is theoretically as well as practically true. There is no exhaustive inventory of all the different ways something can be taught, and we never can tell whether a new approach might not change our whole sense of what's possible at any given age. For example, could six- and seven-year-olds learn differential calculus and relativity physics? I rather suspect they could achieve a mastery of basic concepts if—and the *if* is essential—their teachers had a mastery of calculus and relativity and a knack for introducing new concepts to young children.

Be that as it may, there are too many algebra teachers who, thoroughly dependent upon textbooks, don't know how to lead youngsters through that intriguing world of unknowns and variables. Similarly, there are too many teachers who teach writing but don't ever try to write a story or essay themselves, or who drill students in reading but don't read anything that challenges. This is not entirely the fault of teachers. In most teacher training institutions the emphasis is on discipline, classroom organization, child psychology, and teaching methods. The whole training program is devoted to learning how to wrap a package and practically no attention is paid to what's in it.

I don't believe that most elementary and secondary teachers aren't smart enough to deal with complex ideas and content. Often a life of teaching dulls teachers' minds and drains their energy. A lot of that can be attributed to the almost exclusive concentration of in-service training on teaching methods and psychology. Teachers need a good dose of content every few years; need to become students again and explore areas of knowledge they teach, might like to teach, or are merely curious about. It's easy to burn out if you're not learning and teaching something new periodically in your life. Teachers need to stretch out and touch the world, to forget their authority and allow themselves to be curious children every once in a while.

I've been fortunate in that the content of what I teach has usually interested me almost as much as the growth of my students. One of the powerful incentives for me to be an elementary school teacher is that I can teach anything and everything. University professors often find themselves locked in a field they chose when they were in graduate school. A friend of mine has been teaching eighteenth-century English prose at a major university for twenty-five years. He has reached the point where he hates most of it and spends time parodying what he is supposed to be teaching with a passion. His actual passion is for contemporary radical writing in the United States and Europe. He taught himself Italian and Spanish so he could follow its development, and has become eloquent on the nuances of political and philosophical essays that have emerged from the left wing. For several years now he's requested permission to teach contemporary prose. Unfortunately his department already has its full complement of twentieth-century prose men and women and so he's had to remain discontentedly within his field.

Something in me has always resisted the life of a specialist. I love teaching but need to feel free to teach what I love. That doesn't mean giving up teaching reading, writing, or arithmetic so much as approaching them as techniques that students can master in many different ways and through almost any kind of content. It also means being able to shift priorities to maintain control of a teaching day. The elementary school provides a vehicle to experiment with content and technique that is not usually available to the college teacher.

17.

ORGANIZATION OF CONTENT
AND DEVELOPMENT
OF SOPHISTICATED THINKING

The balance between love of content and love of the process of learning is one that every teacher has to set and reset throughout a career. I don't think I've ever taught a class where one or the other of them wasn't dominant. There were times when I was learning a particular subject, and my teaching was centered around sharing that subject with my students. At other times my focus was on their learning process, and the content became secondary to the thinking skills they were mastering. On reflection, the teachers who excited me the most when I was a student were the content-obsessed ones, though there were two or three teachers whose kindness and personal support gave me the courage and persistence to tackle content I felt I might not be able to master.

The teacher who taught me the most about ways of organizing and communicating content was Lynn Loomis, the chairman of the Mathematics Department when I was an undergraduate at Harvard. My first encounter with him was in a section of Math 1A, the introductory course for majors and non-majors. Mathematics was not my field; philosophy was. Yet mathematical ideas excited me. At high school I enjoyed classes that dealt with mathematical and scientific concepts but had no patience for long calculations, solutions of simultaneous equations, and hours spent in the lab nursing an experiment to fruition.

From the first day of the first class I took with him, Loomis's approach to mathematics was a continual revelation. There was no workbook or textbook. He told the class that we would learn as much algebra and calculus as we could learn. He said that since he didn't know us yet, he had no idea how far the class could go. Even more important for me now, as someone who takes teaching very seriously, he told us he could not assume that we knew anything about mathematics though he presumed that since we had passed our SATs we could add, subtract, multiply, divide, and solve some simple algebraic equations. What he did assume was some intellectual sophistication. His notion of intellectual sophistication is worth examining in some detail.

Sophistication in the sense that Loomis used it does not have to do with the specifics of what one knows. It has to do with how a person uses his or her mind. This encompasses such aspects of thinking as the ability to perceive relationships and to entertain several lines of thought at the same time. It also has to do with the ability to understand complex consequences of simple assumptions as well as to concentrate on an idea for some time, to perform experiments in one's imagination, and to grasp structural properties of whole systems instead of just unrelated facts and concepts. This type of sophistication can manifest itself in social and artistic thought as well as in math and science.

Recently I came upon a wonderful example of intellectual sophistication. I discovered a two-record set called *Head Start: With the Child Development Group of Mississippi*, produced by Asch Records in the late 1960s. The Child Development Group of Mississippi (CDGM) was one of the most effective educational programs in the South that developed during the civil rights movement. The record was made during Head Start classes at CDGM and one can hear the voices of three-, four- and five-year-old children as well as their teachers. One particular band on the record struck me with the sophistication of the teaching and learning involved, though someone outside the black community might fail to pick up on the complexity of imagery and thought the children were mastering. The band begins with a bird call. It is the song of the Mississippi quail, and here is a transcription from the record which illustrates how music, animal sounds, and communal singing can be used as sophisticated teaching tools:

> Anybody ever hear that before? Now, that's the first quail call. And that used to be the signal that our people used to use to steal us away to freedom by way of the underground railroad. Which is another way of sayin' an organization to help us get out of bondage and out of slavery. Now this song is called "The Drinking Gourd." Anybody here ever see a drinking gourd? Well, a drinking gourd is like a dipper that our forebearers used to grow and make, 'cause the white folks wouldn't give us any dippers or pails to drink out of, so we had to make our own. But the song "The Drinking Gourd" is talking about the Big Dipper in the sky. Anybody ever see the Big Dipper at night? Any of you ever seen the Big Dipper? It's a bunch of stars in the sky and in that bunch of stars is a star called the North Star. And our people knew that if they got their eye on that North Star, and just kept on running long enough, they'd make it to Canaan Land. It was too dangerous back then to call it Canada. And it says "When the sun comes back and the first quail calls—" When the sun comes back is in the springtime. And the reason it had to be springtime was because during the winter, it was just too cold 'cause the people who were getting away had to sleep in the fields or forests or stations by the road.

> > O when the sun comes back and the first quail calls
> > Follow the drinking gourd
> > The old man is a-waiting for to carry you to freedom
> > If you follow the drinking gourd.

> Follow the drinking gourd
> Follow the drinking gourd
> The old man is a-waiting for to carry you to freedom
> If you follow the drinking gourd.

And that old man was a-waiting to carry us to freedom had been in the storm a long time an' he finally got his right foot caught in a bear trap that the white folks set to keep us from getting away and to keep people from coming in to help us. But that didn't stop him, he had a nerve of steel, so he got and cut that foot off. That left foot print and that right peg foot print in the sand became one of the most famous signs on the underground railroad. 'Cause our people knew if they went down to the riverside and they saw that left foot print and that peg foot print, they were on the right river and the old man was nearby to lend 'em a helping hand whenever they needed it.

> O well the river bank'll make a mighty good road
> The stars will show you the way.
> Left foot, peg foot.

Three-, four- and five-year-olds who can understand and sing of the quail call, freedom, the relationship of the stars and the drinking gourd, are capable of thinking in sophisticated ways about many other subjects as well.

As this illustration indicates, there are many ways to develop sophisticated thinking. Some people learn to think about other people or manage ideas through sound, color, or the manipulation of visual images or physical objects. They use metaphor to express thought. Others use numbers or words. Some people become sophisticated when they are challenged by more experienced people. Others seem to have a natural sophistication in one or more areas. What has astonished me throughout my teaching career is the number of school failures that are intellectually sophisticated and the number of "good" students who fall apart when any degree of intellectual sophistication is demanded of them.

I remember a particularly dramatic example of the discovery of unexpected intellectual sophistication in one of my schools. It was almost fifteen years ago. I was teaching a writing class in a storefront school and the writer Ishmael Reed asked me to take on a young man who was about to drop out of high school. I did and the first day of class I found myself focusing on Victor's writing and his responses to my comments. I began by talking about metaphor and reading some metaphors drawn from classical poetry. My intent was to break the students free from literal description and encourage them to become more imaginative in their writing. As I presented the metaphors, Victor did what I can only describe as digging them out. He probed into four or five interpretations of each image, modified them, and produced yet other variations in our group writing. All this was done in phrases. Victor didn't talk sentences so much as insights. He understood words with an ease and sophistication I'd never encountered before. Even though he was only fifteen at the time, I insisted after that first session that he teach the class along with me. The poetry he wrote casually during class time was better than any I could possibly produce and his insight into language was as sophisticated as mine. There was no need to pretend that he had to be a student just because he was fifteen.

An example of Victor's sophistication is this poem he wrote and published in a pamphlet called "Papo Got His Gun" the summer before we met:

A Letter to Jose

Jose i know that you would understand
why i have not been able to go to the block
but i have run into some problems
but I'm really O.K.
Joe i been fighting
not the way we used to fight with the Sportsmens

but with words that must be as sharp as blades
you know as well as i know who our enemy is
it isn't just them Jose
they are more and don't let anyone convince you
that they are only white
they are all colors
we have found out the hard way Jose
freezing in those apartments
and playing in deadly streets
and you know how horrible it was when we was jitterbugging
there are people who say my story is dying
but i'm going to stick with it
cause i know you're still in the ghetto
and momma is there
and Tito has been killed by it
i'm not writing much this time
tell all the guys i wrote
tell Carmen not to worry about me.

   The way he ties together street fighting, political struggle, and his struggles as a writer and makes all three levels work together is a good example of what Loomis meant by intellectual sophistication. Now, at thirty, Victor Hernandez Cruz is a distinguished poet whose understanding of language continues to grow and to be transformed into fiction and poetry. Of course, not everyone is a Victor. Still, it's remarkable how young people can become sophisticated when talking and thinking about things that matter to them. I believe that intellectual sophistication can be developed even within the context of an overcrowded, undersupplied, stuffy public school classroom. What is essential is taking time for what the Germans call *Sprache*, which can loosely be translated into English as serious continuing discussion which allows people's voices to develop and be heard.

18.

SPRACHE

Sprache is another way of saying thoughtful speech. Children don't have enough time for discussion and reflection in most American classrooms and therefore don't learn how to speak thoughtfully and sensitively. Teachers are locked into so many structured demands that they have little time to "spare" for this essential aspect of the development of young minds.

The absence of time for informed dialogue and open-ended exploration of ideas is frustrating for people who take teaching seriously. I remember wanting to talk with my students for hours at a time my first few years teaching and being scared about not getting through the curriculum or teaching anything. I couldn't (and still can't) turn the development of sophisticated thinking into a list of ordered behavioral objectives, nor could I tell exactly what each student learned from our conversations. As a beginning teacher I couldn't see the school year as a whole. Each day was a unit, each week a totality. It took years to see how *Sprache* turned into complex learning over the course of the school year and to develop patience based on the knowledge that a lot of time invested in intelligent discussion at the beginning of the school year resulted in students' being able to master the expected curriculum in a critical and thoughtful way at the end of the year. It also took a while to learn how to play a somewhat Socratic role during class discussions in order to get students who are accustomed to giving mechanical and safe responses to teachers' questions to be bold and thoughtful.

One particular conversation is a good illustration of *Sprache* and how it elicits sophisticated thought. I was working with a group of junior high school students. At that time Pink Floyd's "Another Brick in the Wall" was in the top ten and the students wanted to use it for their graduation song. I suggested that before they petition to use the song we go over the words and examine what they're saying about school. One particular stanza stood out in the kids' minds:

> We don't need no education.
> We don't need no thought control
> No dark sarcasm in the classroom
> Teachers leave them kids alone
> All in all you're just another brick in the wall.

The students loved the song and listened to it endlessly whether they got straight A's or chronic F's. It responded to some despair and anger they all felt about their school experiences, though I doubted whether they had articulated what they were responding to. Their reaction to the song was on a gut level, yet the lyrics contained some powerful imagery which could help them think about their schooling in more sophisticated ways. What was the relation between education and thought control? What was "dark sarcasm" and how did it work in the classroom? And what did it mean to conclude that all in all teachers are just another brick in the wall? What wall?

These questions were the basis upon which I built an ongoing discussion of education and its relationship to the wounds suffered by students who are constantly being graded and humiliated into accepting without question what their teachers and textbooks say is true. The discussion of thought control led to a consideration of the kinds of questions teachers and textbooks asked. One of the girls remarked that you never had a need to think because all the questions had right or wrong answers. I pushed and asked what other kinds of questions there were. Someone responded that there were questions that had to do with feelings and opinions. One usually silent and sullen boy added, "And there are questions that don't have answers, like why do we have schools in the first place?" My response was more questions: Did schools always exist? Who created them and how did they come to take the form they currently have?

We even examined a few textbooks and as an exercise rephrased some questions to allow for more open-ended answers. My role in the discussion was to keep the questions going, to help the students think about their answers and imagine other possible answers. It was also occasionally to provide information or change the subject when fatigue set in or a dead end seemed to have been reached. I was trying to awaken dulled minds, to find ways to focus thought and energy and encourage the expression of ideas. The goal was not to reach agreement about answers to my questions. It was to have students develop the habit of raising questions and entertaining a variety of answers.

After our discussion, two groups of students decided as a social studies topic to see how textbooks over the last hundred years treated the issues of slavery and women's liberation. A search in the school and public libraries and a local bookstore turned up history textbooks dating from 1880 to the present and ranging in attitude from racist and anti-suffragette to egalitarian and feminist ones; indeed, there was perhaps an overestimation of the positive effects of civil rights and women's movements. In some ways these latter books were the most interesting to the students. They proclaimed that racial and sexual discrimination had been eliminated in the United States during the sixties and early seventies and were therefore not problems we had to worry about anymore. This was counter to the students' own experience in the eighties. They knew many racists and knew about attempts to re-introduce segregation. Some also knew, from mothers who worked and managed single-parent families, the realities of sexual discrimination.

The results of the groups' research were shared with the rest of us and led us to look with a critical sensibility at the textbook the school was using.

Another part of "Another Brick in the Wall" led to equally interesting discussions and explorations. "Dark sarcasm" turned out to be a problem for all the students. None of them knew exactly what sarcasm was, though they guessed that it had to do with saying nasty things about people. The phrase "dark sarcasm in the classroom" moved the students without their being able to articulate why. The closest they got was that teachers did something evil and unspoken to their students, which hurt a lot. I suggested that someone look up "sarcasm" in a dictionary. They found that according to the *American Heritage Dictionary*, sarcasm was "a sharply mock-ing or contemptuous remark, typically utilizing statements or implications pointedly opposite or irrelevant to the underly-ing purport," and that it was derived from the Greek *sarkazein*, which meant to tear the flesh off a living thing. Rachel, who was having a difficult time in math, immediately volunteered a description of dark sarcasm in the classroom. She said it was like when Mr. Solor, her math teacher, called her his little genius every time he returned her math papers, which always received Ds or Fs. She said it always made her feel naked and ashamed in front of her friends. It was like tearing her flesh off.

Rachel's example led to an extended discussion of the forms and ceremonies of humiliation in school, ranging from teachers' making A students feel guilty and alienated from their friends by holding them up as good examples, to coaches and gym teachers' making fun of slow, fat, or awkward students. The discussion ranged from the specific to the concepts involved and after a few days became very sophisticated as students tried to examine the structure and use of humiliation in controlling thought. This led to the last line: "All in all you're just another brick in the wall." The wall became the symbol of a rigid, unkind system. The teacher was "just another brick" and the students caught on immediately that the police, callous doctors and lawyers, politicians who cared more for money than for people, were also bricks in the wall. The wall itself was a certain kind of society, one that thought control in the schools made it hard to analyze and change.

Toward the end of our series of conversations, one of the girls asked me if the group Pink Floyd had thought all this through when they composed and recorded the song. My response was that I doubted it and wasn't even sure that their interpretation was the same as the musicians'. Many people say and write things whose significance and implications come out only through analysis and questioning.

I was able to talk about "Another Brick in the Wall" with my students because I had made it my business to listen to the records they liked and to take their judgments seriously. I enjoyed some of the music they liked. It's not necessary to enjoy or pretend to enjoy what your students like. It is crucial, however, to respect and know what they enjoy and take seriously, if you are to create serious exchange and encourage their ability to think and express their thoughts. It is also essential to eliminate sarcasm from your own speech. To teach well, you have to listen to your students, to elicit their thoughts and see them struggling with ideas. At the beginning of a school year it is especially important to create time for talk, dialogue, and open-ended inquiries. As you get to know what they know and something of how they think, you'll be able to build a repertoire of basic ideas that interest your class and can lead to complex thinking later on in the year.

19.

ABSTRACTION

Some of the most effective techniques I learned for building a repertoire came from my professor Lynn Loomis's methods of approaching abstract mathematics. As I said, Loomis assumed a certain level of intellectual sophistication for each of his classes. I think what he meant was that the mind had to be trained to think abstractly and that the more abstract and complex the subject, the better shape the mind had to be in. I remember feeling my head hurt when I tried to conceptualize abstract spaces of twenty dimensions and then deduce their properties, or to hold fifteen variables in mind when thinking through a problem. After a while, thinking abstractly became easier. It was just like getting in training to run a marathon or swim a mile. There is pain as the body stretches out, but it gets easier. The same is true for the mind in training.

Loomis let our minds grow, but he also freed us of the burden of having to know particular facts about specific mathematical issues. It didn't matter how or even whether you had acquired any specific mathematical knowledge in the past. His classes freed you of the biases of your educational past and put you directly in contact with the content to be mastered in the present. I've tried to do the same thing throughout my teaching career—that is, teach sophisticated content while assuming minimum background knowledge on the part of my students. The guiding principle for me is to present a subject so that anyone who can think in a fairly complex way can master it, no matter what his or her prior school history has been.

Mathematical theory is an ideal subject to teach without making assumptions about what your students already know. It depends upon the ability to think through a problem and doesn't require much prior factual information. Loomis began, for example, with the basic undefined terms of set theory, like set, element, and operation, and explained them through metaphor and example until we had internalized them. He kept questioning the class and encouraging us to question him. He also assured us that there was no need to rush through the material. Understanding, not speed, was essential. I've always remembered this concern, and I spend a lot of time assessing whether my students understand an idea or a concept and discovering how effective my explanations are.

I also remember a particularly elegant presentation Loomis made of John von Neumann's derivation of all of the natural numbers (the integers including zero) from the sparse notions of a set that contains nothing and an operation that allows one to make sets out of other sets. The emergence of complexity from deceptively simple assumptions and the ability to draw out the consequences of assumptions are beautifully illustrated in this derivation. When I was teaching sixth grade, I wanted my students to understand and use these concepts. I eventually had an opportunity to introduce my class to Loomis's derivation. One of the students had asked what a number really was. She said that the number one couldn't be one doll or one apple or one book and it couldn't be all of them because then it would be three. Doris was always raising interesting questions like that one, sometimes to confuse or challenge me, but mostly because she was an intellectually curious youngster with a very subtle mind. I tried to come up with some explanation that would satisfy Doris and the rest of the class, who quickly understood the paradox of defining numbers that Doris had raised. At first I tried to say that numbers were abstractions, common properties of things, that "oneness" was what was common to all groups that contained only one thing. One of the boys said everybody knew that already, but it still didn't tell them what "one" was. I agreed, and promised to think about the question and do some research on it that night at home and try to answer it the next day.

The class was delighted that I was stumped but even more pleased ~~that I promised to find an answer rather than forget the question.~~ After school, Doris ran up to me at the bus stop and asked me to tell her how to do research so she could answer questions like that for herself. I promised and made the development and answering of difficult questions a theme of part of our work that year.

That night I puzzled over how to define "one." To repeat the New Math textbook definition that the number one was the set of all sets that contained one thing was precisely the begging of the question Doris and the others were challenging. I felt that there was probably no answer that would satisfy my students and decided to explain to them about the intuitive sense we all have about numbers and then show them how mathematicians try to go about formalizing that sense into a model they can use for complex manipulation of simple ideas. I decided to do a version of Loomis's derivation of the natural numbers and explain that mathematicians create models they can manipulate that formalize intuitive ideas about number and space and shape.

The next day I brought a large carton to class and began the day by writing out Doris's question and telling everyone that I was sure they wouldn't all be satisfied with my answer but it was the best I could do. First I asked whether they could tell the difference between three dimes and two dimes, one book and six books. Of course they could, they said, and I explained that the intuitive sense of number came from dealing with experience and learning a language people created to deal with experience. I then asked if that language of number had to be true in every possible world, and Larry, our resident science fiction expert, said he could imagine a world where every time you put two objects together they turned into three objects. In that world there would be no two. Doris objected that there would still be the idea of two even if there were no two objects you could add up to two. Only the rules would have to be different. Adding would somehow have to have a statement like $1 + 1 = 3$.

I jumped in at that point and explained that Doris was doing just what mathematicians do—building models. Sometimes the models are meant to fit our experience, other times they are meant to test out worlds we can only imagine. Then I said that I'd brought with me a physical model of a system my math teacher showed me at college to deal with the numbers we experience in our everyday life. That was the best I could do. I couldn't answer what "one" was but could show how mathematicians dealt with "one" and other natural numbers. Then I opened the carton and took out a smaller carton. Doris opened the smaller carton and found another box inside it. The students took turns until they opened the last of the seven boxes I had nested together. There was nothing in the last box and everybody looked at me for an explanation.

I put the sign for the null set, the set containing nothing, on the board: $\wedge$ Nothing was where the mathematicians began and should be thought of as what is in that last box. Now, if we represent the box by brackets, we can say that one is the box that contains nothing, written $\{\wedge\}$. Two could then be thought of as a box that contained the null set $\wedge$ and our newly constructed number one. Thus, two would be in our simple system {∧, {∧}}. I asked the class what they thought three would be and got {∧, {∧}, {∧, {∧}}}, the right construction with even the right number of brackets. After going up to five, several of the students came up with the insight that a model of all the natural numbers could be built up from nothing and the idea of putting nothing in a box, which was precisely the John von Neumann construction that Loomis had demonstrated.

This example illustrates how much intellectual sophistication can emerge when content is organized so that students are helped to think their way through a problem. Of course, every teacher can't be expected to have my interest in math, and I know my own inadequacies in music and drawing make it unlikely that I would be able to help students think and function in sophisticated ways in these subjects. Still, there is a lot most of us can do in major areas in the curriculum that can lead young children to think. They have to do with

- <u>Organizing content around specific powerful teaching</u> images, ideas, or experiences. These might include:

  in math—infinity, spatial transformation, zero, limits, and curves

  in English and social studies—the themes of loyalty, deception, revolution, affection, wisdom, and wickedness

  in physical education—the idea of the limits of the human body to move at a certain speed or jump a certain height (the study of the change in athletic records for women athletes, for example, can lead to study of the whole question of physical stereotyping).

- <u>Preparing more material than you will be able to use and</u> <u>being prepared to adjust the content to student re-</u> <u>sponses.</u>

- Introducing content with very few specific factual pre-requisites.
- Providing opportunity for lots of talk and experimentation.
- Being willing to approach the content in different ways if your students don't understand your initial presentation.
- Being prepared to give up teaching content that seems currently too remote or difficult for your students and moving on to something else without punishing them.

Dealing with content in these ways demands a lot from teachers. There is research to do and material to prepare and organize. There is also need for a testing period, a time to try out new ideas with children so that you can develop a sense of what initial teaching experiences are likely to be interesting. It took me years to build up enough personal knowledge and gather a library of teaching and research resources to gain some mastery of content. It is sensible to research and plan in a few subject areas at a time and build a teaching repertoire. It's like a musician or actor building up a coherent repertoire over a lifetime. You don't start by learning to play all of Mozart or act in all of Shakespeare on superficial levels. Mastery requires digging in at some place, learning one sonata or role well and slowly developing a repertoire. It's the same with teaching. You have to choose a place, a theme or subject to research, organize and teach (to people of many different ages, if possible) and then spread from there to other areas of the curriculum. That means that for the first few years your teaching will be uneven. You will emphasize some subjects more than others, deal with some in depth and with others superficially, teach some with excitement and ingenuity and others mechanically, to be "gotten through" rather than taught. I don't see any alternative. Nobody starts out as a completely effective and creative teacher. Teaching well is an acquired skill and one has to work at it.

There follow examples in different subject areas of how content might be organized to help students develop thinking skills while mastering some specific content.

20.

APPROACHING
THE SHORT STORY

A sensible way to prepare to teach short story writing is to read lots of short stories. They can range from stories in popular romance and detective magazines to collections of such masters as Kafka, Faulkner, Hemingway, Grace Paley. Go to a bookstore or library, wander around the sections where there are collections of short stories, and buy or check out a half dozen at random. Teaching well requires investing time and sometimes money. Try science fiction, juvenile fiction, classic stories, anything you can get your hands on. A few weeks of reading will do. Read the stories and don't worry about teaching them. It is important to relax and let yourself respond to the material directly, personally, rather than as a prospective teacher of it, which would dampen the pleasure involved in encountering something new on its own terms.

After immersing yourself in stories, you can begin to organize them around certain recurring ideas, images, or experiences. Several years ago, I taught short story writing in a fourth- and a fifth-grade class. I had been struck by how many of the stories I had read were elaborations of an extremely simple idea or story line. A person turns into a bug overnight, an old boxer tries to get the courage to fight one more time, two people sacrifice something they treasure to buy each other birthday presents, former lovers meet for the last time, someone has to tell someone else about a death—such themes are the basis of many short stories. I decided that one way to approach narrative writing was the progressive elaboration of a very simple theme, and began to experiment with this approach. Here are two narratives with some early elaborations:

Bare bones tale 1:
> The man walked into a restaurant. He sat down. He ordered a cup of coffee. He drank it. He paid and left.

Elaboration 1:
> The man looked around, then quickly entered the restaurant. He sat down and mumbled that he wanted a cup of coffee. He gulped it down though it was steaming hot. Then he got up, looked around suspiciously, threw change on the table, and left.

Elaboration 2:
> The man's hat was pulled down over his forehead, his collar was turned up. His eyes darted around as he stepped quickly into the seedy restaurant. He sat down at the counter and mumbled something that sounded like "Coffee black and strong." The counter waitress asked him what was wrong and his only response was another mumbled "Coffee now." He almost grabbed the cup when the waitress brought it, drank it down as if it were a cool glass of white wine, sighed, shoved some coins across the counter, and left as abruptly as he had entered.

Bare bones tale 2:
> They were old friends. They met on the street by accident and were glad to see each other. They went to a restaurant and talked about old times. Then they said good-bye.

Here are some elaborations on this story that were done by fourth graders when I began teaching short story writing:

Student 1:
> Todd, Eric, Lucius. They were old friends. Todd wore blue

pants, a white T-shirt, and a hat. Eric wore blue pants and a green shirt. Lucius wore brown pants and a white T-shirt. They met on the street by accident. They were glad to see each other. They went to a restaurant to talk about old times. After they were done they said good-bye. The next day in the newspaper it said: Lucius was killed. Todd and Eric were sad.

Student 2:

They were very old friends. Their names were Bill Johnson and Pete Randall. One foggy day they met on 5th and Broadway by accident. They were glad to see each other after twenty years. They went to a fancy restaurant to talk about old times. A little while later they felt sad because they had to leave so they said good-bye.

I created about a dozen basic bare bones stories and eventually used six or seven of them. Elaboration on a simple story line was only one approach to writing a short story. It provided a nice introductory warm-up exercise. But playing with these elaborations led me to see how important character, place, and action were in narrative form. I developed a number of other exercises dealing with these aspects of writing short stories, to add to the skills developed in the elaboration exercise. They involved writing character sketches, telephone conversations, fictional diaries, and short intimate conversations. I also decided to concentrate on romantic mystery stories, since the fourth and fifth graders I was going to be working with (one of whom was my son Josh) seemed interested in mystery and romance. I spent time talking informally with the children during their lunch and yard breaks, and they told me they watched mystery programs on TV and had a number of romances going on in their lives. Romantic mysteries united cultural with personal interests and therefore seemed to provide a good starting point to lead them to more sophisticated and interesting literature.

Here are the notes I prepared for myself, which served as lesson plans:

Writing—Middle Grades
October 7, 1980

1. **Create a character sketch of:**
   (a) a mysterious person
   (b) a detective
   (c) a kid who decides to be a detective

   The sketch should include:
   (1) physical description including eyes, hair, body type, way moves
   (2) clothes
   (3) weapons
   (4) psychological makeup and intelligence
   (5) a short account of their past (family, other cases they worked on, etc.)

2. **Write a description of a place where action is to take place.** It could be a house, a town, a city, a future or space environment. It should include:
   (1) what it looked like
   (2) who lived there
   (3) places to hide and places to look for people in hiding
   (4) description of a few people who live there

3. **Do a sketch of a scene between several people where something happens.** This could be a scene where:
   (a) something mysterious happens
   (b) someone asks another person for help
   (c) someone describes something suspicious that has happened to someone else
   (d) one person catches another doing something strange
   (e) one person reveals love (no love) to another
   (f) any other scene you care to write

   Include:
   (1) what people are thinking
   (2) description of people

    (3) description of place where action is happening

    (4) a little bit about why what is happening has occurred

4. Begin a mystery story paying attention to character, place, and action.

I designed all the lessons so that they could be done whether or not you had ever read a short story. I also picked out two stories to reproduce, one by Hemingway and one by Kafka, and prepared to read them in class if the opportunity arose. The Hemingway story ("The Killers") was almost all dialogue and the Kafka ("Josephine the Singer, or the Mouse-folk") almost all description. Hemingway was cold and realistic, Kafka wild and surrealistic. I hoped an occasion would arise to read both stories and discuss their contrasts with the classes I was working with. As it turned out, I never got to read either story, though they became the basis for a short story unit I did with some junior high students the next year.

The elaborations and sketches of scenes, characters, and actions worked out quite well. However, about a quarter of the students, after going through the exercises, made it clear that they didn't want to write detective romances. They preferred science fiction, swashbuckling adventure, and violent love stories. Here are two samples of the stories that resulted; they were edited and revised several times. I set up the class to work like a publishing house: We had a production team, a number of editorial boards, several copy editors (these were, not surprisingly, the best spellers), and a sales production and distribution group.

Will Minnie Win Harper?

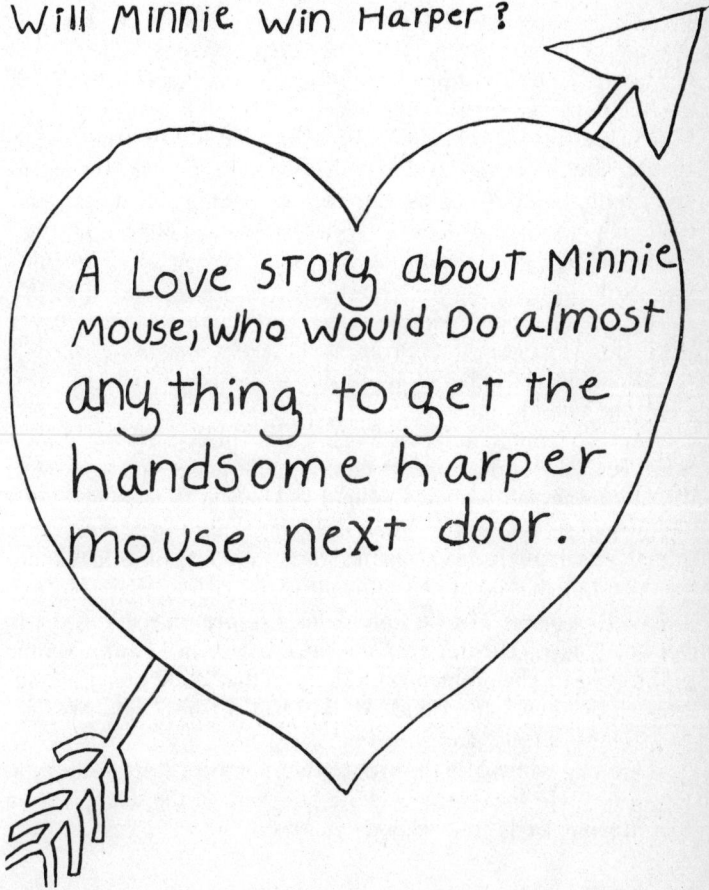

A Love story about Minnie Mouse, who would Do almost anything to get the handsome harper mouse next door.

THE LOVELY MINNIE MOUSE
by
Amanda Leary

Minnie Mouse peeked out of the mouse hole and liked what she saw. What beautiful scenery! There were mountains (molehills), in the background, beautiful colored trees (flowers), and the sun was shining down on Minnie's shoulders.

Minnie went into her room and looked at her pretty image in the mirror. She was a little field mouse with rosy cheeks and a little red mouth. She was wearing her favorite outfit, a pink dress with a matching hat, coat, and parasol. She thought she was the prettiest mouse in the world (which to her was Mr. and Mrs. Meenie's backyard).

Just then, Mother Mouse walked in (Minnie's Mom), "If you don't stop looking in the mirror, I will take it away from you!"

Minnie looked at her mother's slim figure in the doorway, "Yes, Ma," she said gloomily.

One of Minnie's problems was her little brother, Bobby Mouse. Everytime she said anything, Bobby would make a joke out of it. He was always following her around and bugging her. Bobby was a sloppy mouse, his fur was always dirty, his clothes were always torn and everywhere he went he made a mess. Minnie hated her brother, but she didn't like to admit it.

Another one of Minnie's problems was mealtime. Everyone in her family loved cheese, everyone, that is, except Minnie. Minnie hated cheese. The problem with that was that all they ever ate was cheese. So, every mealtime, Minnie had to sneak into Mr. and Mrs. Mouse's cellar and steal their rice.

One day while Minnie was getting her rice, her brother followed her. He sneaked up behind her, and, in the deep voice of Mr. Meenie, said, "Just what do you think your doing stealing my rice!"

Minnie jumped with fright, turned around and ran. When Minnie got home, she heard Bobby telling his friend what he did. Minnie was furious. She went and told her mother and father. They gave Bobby a good whipping.

Minnie Mouse loved to play dress-up with her friend, Molly Mouse. They loved to dress up like human beings. Usually, when they dressed up like people, they put mouse-made wigs on their heads and hid their ears with fancy hats with tiny flowers on them. They wore long black dresses. They wore bark with a string around it for high heels and juice from a rose for lipstick and rouge. They used bluebells for eye shadow and coal for mascara.

Sometimes Bobby played dress-up with them. When he did he wore his satin tophat and his tie and black pants. He also wore a white shirt and black jacket and boots. They all looked so cute when they played dress-up.

Bobby had a mad crush on Molly, and everytime Molly was Mother when they played dress-up, Bobby asked to be Father.

One day Bobby asked Molly to go with him. Molly said she would be delighted to and Minnie gasped with amazement. All these years she thought Molly hated Bobby, but now she knew she was wrong.

"How in the world could anyone love sloppy Bobby when she could stare at the handsome Harper Mouse next door!" she thought.

I think it is time I told you all about Harper Mouse, so, I will. Harper was ten mouse-years old. So were Minnie and Molly, and Bobby was nine. Harper was very handsome! He had shiny brown fur. It was so smooth that Minnie always longed to touch it. He had long, silvery white whiskers and sparkling white teeth. His blue eyes glistened in the sun. He dressed nicely and he was always very neat (for a mouse anyway.)

Now that Molly and Bobby were going together, they didn't pay any attention to Minnie anymore. Minnie grew sad and lonely. She wished she would also have a boyfriend so she wouldn't be lonely anymore.

One day while she was sitting on a toadstool crying, Harper came and sat beside her.

"What's the matter?" Harper asked.

Minnie told him all about how lonely she was and how she needed someone to keep her company.

"I think I can solve your problem with one question," said Harper shyly.

"What's the question?" she asked.

"Will you go with me?" he asked.

"Yes, yes, yes, yes, yes!" she screamed.

Minnie was very happy with Harper. He took her for rides on his motorcycle, in his airplane, and in his balloon. Soon Minnie found out there was a lot more to the world than Mr. and Mrs. Meenie's backyard!

Years went by and the two lovers were still going together. They were now thirteen mouse-years old. Molly and Bobby were also together but never in the history of mice could anyone be a happier couple than Minnie and Harper.

One day Mr. and Mrs. Meenie bought a little baby duckling. He was a little yellow duckling with soft fur. He was so adorable! Mrs. Meenie named him Fluff. After awhile Fluff got out of his cage outside and began to wander around looking for a friend.

Soon he found Minnie Mouse making a daisy hat for herself. When Fluff saw her he was delighted. "Hi," he said.

Minnie jumped with a start. "Oh, hello," she said when she saw the duckling.

Minnie and Fluff instantly became friends. Minnie gave Fluff the daisy hat and Fluff let Minnie ride on his back all the way home to Minnie's house.

Minnie and Harper now had a home of their own and they invited Fluff to live with them.

One day when Minnie was twenty-one mouse-years old, she found out that she was pregnant. They were so excited. Four more months until the babies were due; three months; two months; one month; two days!!

One day Minnie started getting pains in her belly. She decided it was time for her to have the babies. Out came six cute little mice.

"Mommy, Mommy," they all cried and jumped on Fluff.

"No, you sillies, that's your Mommy," said Fluff.

"Oh," said the mice, and jumped on Minnie. When they found out that Harper was their father, they jumped on him.

Minnie, Harper, Fluff, Mary, Mark, Marie, Jimmy, Larry, and Tiny all lived happily ever after.

THE END

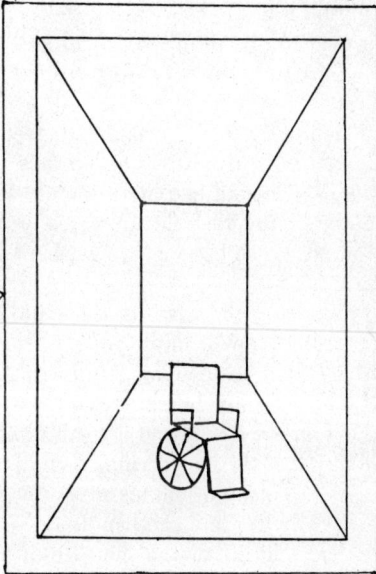

Better Than Coping

By Elana Gerstein

CHAPTER I

I woke up in the morning to hear a crying sound coming from my mother's bedroom. Could my mother really be crying? I didn't know what to think. I called to my Mom but there was no answer.

I slowly sat up, put on my slippers and crawled over to my wheelchair, once I was at the wheelchair, I pushed it over to the bed and helped myself into the chair using the bed as support. I wheeled my chair over to my Mom's door and knocked, I heard a weak little, "Hello," from my mother, so I pushed open the door and went through it.

My Mom had definitely been crying, her pretty green eyes were all wet and her brown hair stuck to her face because of the wetness. Otherwise, she looked like her same old self. I was very worried, because something terrible must really be wrong, especially for my Mom to cry, so I asked, in a weaker voice than hers, what the matter was.

She said that I might as well know, since I would have to sooner or later. She told me about how a couple of days before she had had a bad pain in her chest and was coughing and weak. She had gone to the doctor and he had checked her and tested her. He was sure it was pneumonia. He told her to rest and not work hard at anything.

When she told him that she had a crippled child who needed to be taken care of, with lots of attention, his answer was, "Take her to a relative until you are better and can handle her."

After my Mom had told me that, at first I didn't say anything, but then I burst into tears, crying, "I don't want to leave you Mommy! Please, stay with me!"

My mother tried to ignore me and just said that the only relatives I had were my grandparents and that she had already planned for me to be with them tomorrow, they would come and get me at 12:00.

She reminded me not to feel bad if they weren't used to my handicap. I said that of course I wouldn't, but I wasn't positive.

The rest of the day my Mom and I spent all our time together, laughing in bed, since my Mom needed rest. Then, at night, my Mom sat by me and waited until I fell asleep.

In the morning, when I got up, I didn't complain about anything, I just packed. When my grandparents came, I just said goodbye to my Mom, knowing that she loved me very much.

So, I set off to my grandparents in a green Toyota, and I found that almost everything in their house was green, green, green!

CHAPTER II

By the time we got there, it was dark, so I didn't get to look around at the house, I was shown to my room. In the morning I would unpack, but right now I was. exhausted. My grandfather had made sure that my room was downstairs so that I could function on my own.

Once I was in bed my grandfather came to say goodnight. He told me a story about when he was a little boy. He had been in a play and was about to say something, when all of a sudden, his little sister, who was four, said, "Hi, Peter!" then waved. He was so shocked and embarrassed that he started to crack up. It had been a disaster, all because of his darn sister. My grandfather and I laughed and talked about it even though I was tired, but actually I really wasn't so tired.

Soon it was time for him to go. When he left, I thought that my grandmother would come, so I waited and waited and after about fifteen minutes of waiting, I started getting tired again. I didn't understand why she hadn't come. Then I realized that she hadn't talked to me the *whole* trip. I wondered why?

All of a sudden I heard my grandparents voices. I wasn't sure, but I thought I made out my grandfather calming grandma down. Then I heard grandma say that it wasn't fair that I was crippled, and why did it have to be *her* granddaughter.

After I heard her say that, I started thinking she must feel so sorry for me. She must think I can't do anything! I fell asleep thinking that I would show her, She would see that I was all right!

The next morning my grandmother came into my room to help

me dress. She seemed to hesitate until I said to come on in. Then I remembered that I was to show her I wasn't helpless. So I picked up my pants and put them on my bed, then I lay down and pushed myself into them (it was hard, but I needed to do it.) She was stunned, and asked if I was all right. I said I was.

Through the whole day, whenever I could, I would take care of myself without help. At lunch, when my grandparents were busy, I decided to make lunch. I would make a tuna-fish sandwich. So I took out a can of tuna, poured the oil out, and put it in a bowl. Next I added mayonnaise and chopped celery.

By the time the tuna was mixed, all I needed was the bread. I remembered my grandmother getting it out from a high cupboard. It was the cupboard closest to the dishwasher. I strained and tried to get it, but, I just *couldn't* reach it! I was getting all frustrated when my grandmother opened the kitchen door to come in. Oh, no! Now my surprise was ruined.

Instead, my grandmother seemed very pleased, and said that this was such a *nice* surprise. I beamed with pride and happiness. I thought to myself, "Hey, I really did do it!"

My grandma and I ate together and she said that it was delicious. Later my grandfather came in and he was surprised, too.

After we ate, the three of us played monopoly, it was fun. From then on my grandmother didn't think of me as poor and helpless. She realized that I could do many things.

Now I live back with my Mom again, but still my grandmother and I write to each other, and are very close. In fact, my grandmother is working in a hospital helping handicapped children like me.

21.

THE MIGRATING EYE
AND OTHER
POWERFUL IDEAS

There are many powerful mathematical and scientific ideas that young children can master. Yet where is it possible for a teacher to encounter these ideas if they are not in the set curriculum, not part of teacher training, and not taught or discussed by one's colleagues? I am sorry to make learning to teach well seem like such a lonely activity, but it has been that way for me. For over twenty years now, I've tried to talk with colleagues and administrators about educational ideas and things that have a chance of interesting and challenging students, and have generally received stares of incomprehension. It wasn't so much that the educators didn't like me or my ideas as that they had settled into the established curriculum and it had settled into them. Teaching meant performing a series of tasks during a set time without losing control. The teacher as skilled craftsperson or creative artist was not part of the image they had of themselves.

Still, there are teacher artists and craftspeople who spend their whole careers seeking for interesting material to share with their students and aren't content to teach the same thing year after year. They are learners and researchers themselves, people whose minds are as active as they hope each student's mind will become. In talking to many of these teachers I discovered that we had independently developed similar ways to encounter new ideas and material. One of the simplest and most effective is to ask people for help—librarians, booksellers, college professors, corporate researchers, and workers of all sorts. Asking people you don't know to share their knowledge and resources requires some courage, and yet once you do it and get a generous response it seems natural. Once when I wanted to find out about RNA and DNA, I happened to drive past a genetics lab. On a whim, I pulled into the lab's parking lot and went inside. The secretary asked me what I wanted and I blurted out, "A scientist who can help me. I teach down the street and don't know much about modern genetics." The secretary immediately introduced me to a young scientist, who took me around, gave me pamphlets and catalogues, and invited me to bring some of my students by so she could give them a demonstration of how to make DNA. This experience led me to seek other opportunities to learn and accumulate information and contacts to share with my students. Over the years I've visited animation studios, TV and radio stations, print shops, recording studios, and dozens of other places where people worked and had information and resources to share with young people. Not all my visits were pleasant. I got rebuffed or treated rudely at least as many times as I was welcomed, and came to look upon a rejection as just part of the work of gathering teaching resources.

Another way to gather resources is by subscribing to specialty magazines such as *Scientific American, Science, Natural History*, etc., and reading as much as you can understand and skimming the rest for ideas and directions to explore. It's easy to read *Natural History*, though not always easy to read *Scientific American* and sometimes impossible to follow articles in *Science*. Yet they and other professional magazines are constant sources of powerful teaching ideas and images. Recently, for example, *Scientific American* ran an article on the eyes of flounders. It seems that flounders are born with eyes on both sides of their heads and that as they mature one eye migrates across the head so that adult flounders have both their eyes on the same side. There are some right-eyed flounders and some left-eyed flounders because the eyes can migrate in either direction. I'm not sure that I followed the complexities of the explanation of the phenomena in the magazine, but I knew I had a rich teaching image that could lead, say, from a discussion of the variety of fish to the adaptation of a living creature to its environment to *The Voyage of the Beagle* and a historical consideration of how Darwin came to formulate *The Origin of Species*. I also knew that the idea would be as intriguing to first and second graders as to junior and senior high school students. What I didn't know and what makes teaching so challenging is where such a powerful image would lead a particular group of students. That suspense about how far an idea can be extended in a given context is one of the things that's kept me teaching.

In the case of the migrating eye, it was possible to do a direct investigation of dozens of flounders and see how they changed as they grew. I live a few miles from the Pacific Ocean and many of our students are skilled fishers. They know where to get flounders and so we had lots of specimens to observe. The flounder is a strange-looking creature. It is a bottom fish and somewhere in the course of its evolution the flounder found an advantage in flipping on its side and hugging the bottom. One side became its underside and the other its top. In the course of that transformation, one eye migrated to the topside. However, as one of my junior high students pointed out, the change took place in a strange way, since it didn't happen once and for all and became an inherited characteristic of flounders. Instead, each individual flounder goes through that change in its own lifetime. Why? We could only speculate and in the course of our spinning out theories the question arose whether other creatures went through changes in development that seemed to recapture major changes in the species they belonged to. The obvious example was the human embryo with it gills and tail. Examining flounders led to a study of human embryology even though, as one teacher pointed out to me, embryology isn't a junior high school topic. I've always refused to accept such restrictions. There are no junior high school or elementary school topics; there are only ideas that children should be encouraged to examine when they encounter them. It doesn't make any difference whether they will be expected to deal with similar material at other times during their school career. Embryology, for example, can be studied in kindergarten, in third grade, in junior high, and in high school without ever exhausting the richness of the subject. I believe one of the most important tasks of becoming a decent teacher is to free oneself of the notion that one must teach a set curriculum, and to adopt the idea that the growth of the mind and the development of thought, imagination, and sensibility are the main responsibilities of teachers in all grades and subject areas.

22.

TEACHING *MACBETH*
AND THE CLASSICS

Recently I've become interested in using classical literature
and theater as vehicles for the exploration of such ideas as
power, authority, independence, and the development of
love. About ten years ago, most of my work in literature and
theater centered about student writing and improvisation.
I've seen wonderful material created, but have begun to feel
that student work needs a classical and historical foundation in
order to achieve greater maturity and scope. Most student
work derives from a combination of personal experience and
models drawn from movies, TV, and popular novels. Even
the best of that work can benefit from the complexity of plot
and depth of characterization and imagery of classical theater
and literature. I don't mean by this, however, that we should
force certain works upon students or reinstitute slavish memorizing of the sort my father was exposed to. The only thing he
remembered from high school English was a phrase from a
poem by Milton he was forced to memorize: "In Stygian caves
forlorn." He told me he never forgot those words because
neither he nor any of his friends had the slightest idea of what
it meant and they turned it into a Yiddish phrase roughly
equivalent to "Don't pay any attention to the nonsense he's
talking." Once I heard my father say of an old school friend

who liked to talk but didn't say much, "He's in Stygian caves forlorn again."

However, Milton and Shakespeare, Aristophanes, Rabelais, Joyce, and hosts of other authors are full of life, language, and insight that young people should know, especially given the shallow media language that dominates their experience. Unfortunately classics are usually introduced by reciting their credentials rather than their themes. I've heard *Hamlet* introduced to a groaning class of junior high students as the world's greatest play by the world's greatest playwright. I remember feeling trapped as a sophomore in high school when I was forced to read *Macbeth* and write about how good it was. The goodness I had to discuss overrode my ability to concentrate on the play itself and discover whatever it had to teach me and how it might move me. I've thought about my sophomore *Macbeth* because last summer I decided to do a production of *Macbeth* at our summer school with seven-to-fourteen-year-old children.

In the previous three summers we'd done *Midsummer Night's Dream*, *Antigone*, and *Tartuffe*. The plays were chosen because the first one portrayed adolescent love, the second female defiance of male authority, and the third religious hypocrisy. It was my way of helping students act their way through an understanding of major issues in their lives and in our culture. Last summer seemed right for *Macbeth*, since greed and obsession with power characterizes our recent rulers.

It was a pleasure to be doing *Macbeth* at our summer school and not in the local public school. I have become increasingly weary of classroom teaching as my love affair with teaching and learning has deepened. The tension between having to teach a class during certain times of day and in certain subject areas while knowing that your students would grow more in freer learning situations and with more challenging materials is something every serious teacher I've known has faced in midcareer. If we are to maintain our commitment to public education, will we ever be free to follow our instincts and explore teaching, or do we have to finish our careers still in a classroom chained to a curriculum?

I've made my own decisions and friends have made very different ones. My decision was to pursue a joint career, writing to support myself and teaching in public schools occasionally, but also establishing a place to teach and work with other teachers, where we are free to create the conditions of our work. During the school year I try to push the limits of what can be done in our local public schools. Summer school is different. It's time to teach seriously and therefore time to play.

The usual distinction between work and play that exists in our society dissolves for me when I feel I'm teaching well. All the children are working hard and enjoying what they're doing at the same time. So am I. The Italians have a word they've applied to the serious play involved in learning. They call it *giuoco*. Daniel Tutolo, of Bowling Green State University in Ohio, described his encounter with *giuoco* during a visit to Italy:

> With the cooperation of the Italian Cultural Institute of New York City, I visited nine schools in Milan and Bologna and interviewed over 55 teachers and administrators at all levels, preschool through university. I was attempting to determine the philosophy, methodology, and materials used in the beginning reading process in Italy.
>
> Many of the teachers interviewed used the word *giuoco* in conversation. This concept seemed to be central in the minds of teachers as they explained the beginning reading/writing process. I asked Dr. Cesare Scurati of Catholic University of Milan to explain the concept. "You must understand Italian culture. It is different from the culture you know in America. In the Italian culture there *is not a clear differentiation between work and play*. The definition of *giuoco* in a dictionary is *play*, but not in

the recreational sense. *Giuoco means extension of the lesson*. Apparently this idea originates from the ~~Froebelian notion~~ *that play is the work of children*.

The concept of *giuoco* is an interesting one easily found in the Italian culture. For adults as well as children *giuoco* is a prelude to learning. Italians stop in local coffee shops, called bars, for morning espresso. Customers stand at the counter and continuously banter among themselves and with the bartender, discussing social, political, and economic issues. Voices become animated, a tone of lightness and play pervades. Yet the discussions lead to important conclusions. The Italians are "giuocoing"—in this case, to share the news of the day.

An elderly Bolognese woman had been invited to school to talk to the children about her childhood in the city. She wore the traditional local costume, with a bright yellow bandana around her head. She sat erect in her chair as she recounted the great times children had had at the many festivals held throughout the year. After she left, the teacher led a discussion of dialect differences and the need to respect the languages of all. With a little direction on the part of the teacher, students volunteered to dramatize the visit by the old woman. The children found a bright colored dress in the costume box and a bandana materialized from somewhere. One second-grade girl role-played the experience; after the simulation the teacher led a discussion.

The only counterpart to giuocoing in the United States is the concept of informal dramatics including dramatic play, dramatization of literature, and role playing. Yet I am unhappy with this analogy. Giuocoing seems to be much more spontaneous than informal dramatics. In the United States, drama, even informal drama, is often an adjunct to the teaching/learning experience, while in Italy it seems to be an integral part. Few lessons are complete without giuocoing.

Contrast this with the American culture, where play is rigidly separated from work. Parents send their children to school to work, not to play. Teachers often support this idea and report the *work* schedule to parents at open houses and conferences. ~~But play is an integral part of~~ learning—not play in the recreational sense, but play as an ougrowth of experience. Certainly early-childhood educators in the U.S. have never lost sight of the value of play. Yet I wonder whether this is true in our elementary schools. Perhaps our penchant for work and the work ethic has made us lose sight of the value of play.

At any rate, in Italy, children's *giuoco* is pleasurable, yet meaningful in learning to read and write.

Last summer, producing and directing *Macbeth* with a group of some forty-five youngsters was *giuoco* for me and I hope for my students as well. I chose *Macbeth* not only because the abuse of power is something young people need to think about, but also because several friends of mine said that it was impossible to do Shakespearean tragedy with actors who weren't at least in high school. I love to try what's impossible and so took up the challenge of *Macbeth*. However, I knew that we could not do the entire play, word for word, since we would have only an hour and a half a day for two weeks to rehearse. During the winter I thought about *Macbeth* occasionally, but it wasn't until I encountered an ad in the *New York Times Magazine* that read "Macbeth lives on in story, but Cawdor Castle lives on in fact," and had a photo of Hugh Vaughn, sixth earl of Cawdor, posed in front of Macbeth's Cawdor Castle, that I began to work seriously on planning the play. The photo of the castle made Macbeth's world come alive for me as it did for my student actors during the summer. It gave a scale and shape to Macbeth's world.

I began gathering resources as well as reading and rereading Shakespeare's play to prepare for writing my own shortened version. A trip to a store in San Francisco that sold Scottish imports provided with me historical, clan, and tartan maps of Scotland as well as two ties, one with the tartan of clan Macbeth the other with that of clan Macduff. Throughout summer camp I wore the Macbeth tie and the set designer wore Macduff's tie. Several students brought in ties that had their family tartans and the whole camp had a distinctly Scottish flavor. Our music teacher and I did some research on the

Scottish Highland games and most of our physical activities became centered around caber and stone throwing, clog dancing, Highland wrestling, tug-of-war, and other Scottish games.

I also bought a copy of *Macbeth: The Making of a Film*, by Clayton Hutton (London: Max Parrish Books, 1960) and of the Caedmon recording of *Macbeth* with Anthony Quayle, Gwen Ffrangçon-Davies, and Stanley Holloway. The photos in the book, taken from the film version of *Macbeth* with Judith Anderson and Maurice Evans, provided the students with a sense of the story line of the play. I didn't expect seven- or eight-year-olds to read *Macbeth* or even my script version of the play, and copies of the movie stills gave them enough sense of the whole to see where their roles fitted in.

I listened to the records dozens of times just to get a sense of the rhythms of the language and of the different voices in the story. By the time camp began, I had shaped a thirty-six page script of which ten pages were mine and twenty-six Shakespeare's. I kept all the main speeches, every character, and the entire roles of the witches and Hecate. We held tryouts for the play the first afternoon of school and over thirty youngsters showed up. After looking through the pictures and talking about the story line, I tried to explain the main themes—power, magic, revenge—and informally went through the whole story, sketching in all the roles myself.

I like to review the story with students first, giving them a sense of what to expect from the material. The language of Shakespeare, for example, is difficult for American youngsters, but accessible and moving if they understand the story and the context before trying to get through it. I wanted my students to feel the agony of Macbeth, the pain of Macduff, the wicked playfulness of the witches and Hecate, and the greed and madness of Lady Macbeth. By the time I had run through the story, most of the kids had decided which parts they wanted to try out for. My intent was to give everyone a role he or she could pull off and as many lines as could be handled without embarrassment. I had my first version of a script but was willing to add, subtract, or rewrite parts and lines according to the strengths and weaknesses of the cast. In good Shakespearean tradition, I felt free to play with the play so long as the story and the integrity of the language were maintained. After the play was cast and rehearsed for a week, I also planned to give all the actors tapes of their roles taken from the Caedmon recording so that they could hear a professional performance of it. However, it was essential to let the actors come to their own terms with their roles, and help me modify the script to make them comfortable, before they heard the professionals. I wanted to avoid imitation and make it possible for students to learn from great actors rather than imitate them.

Selecting the boy to play Macbeth was easy. Only one person tried out. Lady Macbeth was much more difficult. There were a dozen girls who wanted the role. I asked each of them to improvise a scene where Lady Macbeth is sleepwalking and sees the blood of Duncan on her hands. Half of them were wonderful, so that it was almost impossible to decide which rendering was best. The other kids helped me out. There was one girl, a very good actress, who would be too old to come back next year, while everyone else would be returning. Why not simply give the part to her since she wouldn't have a chance for a starring role again? I agreed and Aurora became a splendid Lady Macbeth.

Choosing Aurora solved more problems. All the other candidates wanted speaking roles, and it occurred to me on the spot that there was no reason to have three witches in the play instead of six or seven or eight. The more witches, the more of Shakespeare's language could be used, given that each actor would have to memorize fewer lines. Out of the twelve girls who tried out for Lady Macbeth we ended up with seven witches, Hecate, Lady Macbeth's serving woman, Macduff and Banquo (boys and girls alike could try out for any part in the play), and Lady Macbeth—all costumed and speaking roles. We also ended up using considerably more of Shakespeare's language than I had expected.

During the first week, we went through the script and also improvised the scenes so that if anyone forgot lines they would know where they were in the play and could fake it. Throughout the rehearsals of the production—which turned out to be wonderful despite missed cues and an occasional wrong entrance—I tried to stress that we were involved in working theater. What I meant was that changes could be made in the script, the casting, the characterizations, the sets, as the whole developed. We were creating a play even though the script was basically Shakespeare's. In fact, the last two days before the performance, several shy younger children came to rehearsal and asked if they could have small parts, the kind that involved costumes and no more than two or three sentences. I didn't have to do anything, since the cast by then knew exactly how to make small modifications without causing major disruptions and wrote the six new characters in themselves.

I've spent time describing our production of *Macbeth* because it is one of the most vivid examples I've known of teaching freely and yet attending to the serious content and the demanding and remote language of classical literature. I've been involved with what has been called open or progressive education for over twenty years and found these concepts frequently misunderstood. One can teach Shakespeare, microbiology, computer math, as well as simple reading, writing, and arithmetic, in open ways that lead to understanding, mastery, and occasionally love of the subject itself. To teach in an open way does not mean the loss of content, the indulgence of the whims of students, or the avoidance of complexity. On the contrary, it implies control of content, and the ability to deal with new and difficult ideas and concepts—in other words, the development of sophisticated thinking.

23.

KNOWING
HOW TO SET
PROBLEMS

Recently my wife, Judy, showed me a quote from Freeman Dyson's *Disturbing the Universe*, which eloquently describes a major characteristic of teaching well. Dyson is describing his first encounter with Hans Bethe, a Nobel Prize physicist, who was to direct his studies:

> When I arrived at Cornell and introduced myself to . . . [Bethe], two things about him immediately impressed me. First, there was a lot of mud on his shoes. Second, the other students called him Hans. I had never seen anything like that in England. In England, professors were treated with respect and wore clean shoes.
>
> Within a few days Hans found me a good problem to work on. He had an amazing ability to choose good problems, not too hard and not too easy, for students of widely varying skills and interests. He had eight or ten students doing research problems and never seemed to find it a strain to keep us busy and happy. He ate lunch with us at the cafeteria almost every day. After a few hours of conversation, he could judge accurately what each student was capable of doing. It had been arranged that I would only be at Cornell for nine months, and so he gave me a problem that he knew I could finish within that time. It worked out exactly as he said it would. (New York: Harper & Row, 1979. P. 47.)

Although Bethe was working with postdoctoral students on a one-to-one basis, his teaching techniques were not substantially different from what can happen on any level and in a group as well as an individual situation. Talking with students and discovering their current level of sophistication and interests are the basic diagnostic tools of good teaching. Being able to set challenges that are appropriate to these levels and then provide students with resources, hints on occasion, and personal support are what make it possible to turn this diagnostic information into rich learning experiences.

I remember a striking example of how Bethe's technique worked while I was teaching kindergarten and first grade. We were studying insects and one of the girls brought me a spiderweb that she found on a fence outside our room. She had carefully folded the web onto a piece of paper and offered it during lunch break. Donna said that she was afraid of spiders but loved their webs. She wondered how spiders made them. Her mother was a handweaver and Donna had been around looms and fibers most of her life. She had also done some simple weaving in our class, but she said she still couldn't understand how webs worked. I suggested that she try to make one and also try to study all the webs she could find. She asked if several of her friends could work with her, and together they began a study of web making.

Donna pursued the question of how webs were made for at least a month. I helped in an informal way by providing books on spiders, suggesting that the group build a terrarium with branches and leaves similar to the ones they found that had spiders' webs (one of the boys captured a spider and put it inside, and we watched a web develop), and that they place themselves in the role of spiders rather than observers. The group discovered that there was an incredible variety of spiderwebs and that spiders didn't start from the middle and weave out in concentric circles, as the children had originally thought. They discovered how threads are led from twig to twig, creating a framework (a warp, perhaps) that made it possible to weave the rest of the web.

Donna kept pursuing the question of web making long after the other students had grown bored and moved on to other things. It was her problem but we all learned from it, myself included (I've become a web aficionado through Donna's efforts).

Setting problems for individuals or small groups of students can be a problem in itself. Does one change direction every time one perceives a new interest or discovers something that motivates a student? Clearly a classroom teacher can't do that and stay sane and focused. There is a tension between following students' interests and ideas and maintaining a coherent program within a class so that all the students have an opportunity to gain artistic, intellectual, and mechanical skills. I've approached this essential educational tension in a number of different ways over the years and don't believe there's any single ideal solution to balancing personalized learning with helping everyone master the content and skills you believe are needed at that stage of development. Sometimes you have to hold a class together and focus on the same theme or subject. This is particularly true with a passive group of students who need the teacher or the content to be the primary motivating force. Other times (especially if you know all the students and have worked with them before), all you have to do is discover what they are planning to do and become a resource and an occasional gadfly, presenting new ideas, playfully responding to students' work, and helping them perceive some of the more complex implications of questions they've raised.

There are also times when you have to mix and match, to make exceptions and change your own perceptions of what might be best for your students. I learned this quite forcibly from Robby Stuart, one of the students at the Berkeley public alternative high school Other Ways, which I directed and taught in during the late 1960s. We had a wide-ranging, open program. Students could choose their courses, could ask for or initiate new courses, and even had a voice in staff selection. Our goal was to have all of our students read, write, do math and art, and think on sophisticated levels, but we allowed for many different ways of reaching these goals. All students had to choose four classes a day, though, and were expected to stick with them.

Robby came to Other Ways after being thrown out of high school and chased by truant officers for a month or two. His goal in life was to become a saxophone player and he simply had refused to take the classes in math, English, history, etc., that the high school required of him. He went to school for the music periods and stopped going when the administration prohibited him from doing so until he passed the other subjects.

As he put it, he was "run into" Other Ways. He had been delighted to stay home, playing his saxophone and listening to records all day long. When he showed up at our school, he explained his situation and asked me to find a way for him to spend all his time with music. I told him about our four class requirements, about the things he had to do in order to spend time with his sax. I also tried to persuade him that we were groovy, open, friendly, creative, and he looked at me harshly and said, "All I want to do is learn to play saxophone well. I need time and music and music teachers. That's all."

Something in me said that if we couldn't provide Robby with what he needed and articulated, then no matter how open we said we were, we were identical in substance to the high school that had pushed him out.

Sometimes it is simply necessary to break one's own rules in the service of the students, no matter how much embarrassment and seeming loss of authority it causes.

I gave in to Robby, but not completely. If he wanted to spend all his time with music, that was fine. However, we came up with a plan for him to study the history of the saxophone and other reed instruments, to learn to compose and transpose music, to acquire minimal skills on the piano, and to provide a tape of his original compositions as a thesis for graduation. I gave in but in a challenging way. If he wanted to learn music, my feeling was that he should do it in a serious manner, and he didn't resist at all. If he had, my response would probably have been to question his commitment to the instrument and to music. Sometimes young people pretend to be interested in something in order to escape doing things that bore them. More often they are serious but don't believe that teachers will ever help them. A major part of my growth as a teacher has consisted in sorting out jive from seriousness and learning how to break the rules creatively so that young people can learn what they love in depth and without harassment.

24.

CONTENT

AND DISCIPLINE

I don't have the heart to punish children and yet often find myself in situations where I have to be a disciplinarian. Two children are fighting and they must be separated. One child is making such a fuss that he or she has to be stopped. Someone is trying to destroy an expensive piece of equipment. The class bully is picking on the class victim. Someone is throwing spitballs. Someone else is copying. What to do? During my first years of teaching, I was never certain about how to handle instances of disruptive behavior. Sometimes I grabbed a child roughly or screamed. Other times I tried to use my eyes and say nothing or even called a neighboring teacher or assistant principal to help me out. I threatened bad grades or phone calls to parents. At first I was emotionally involved in my students' misbehavior and took it as both a personal affront and a sign of my weakness. After a while I came to see my involvement and anger as silly. Here I was almost twice the size of my students, yelling at them and feeling threatened by their behavior. As my own confidence in the classroom grew, I saw my disciplinary role more and more as theater, as mock anger and pretend toughness. I began to be able to stop fights, control mischief, eliminate bullying, neutralize copying, prevent destruction, and tell a joke at the same time. There were a few tricks to learn, such as separating any kids who were fighting from the rest of the children, or rewriting exams so that students were encouraged to collaborate. Surprisingly, the angriest of youngsters cool down quickly when there are no friends around to egg them on or witness their potential humiliation, and those most intimidated by grades love to work with others. Another trick I learned was to grab a typewriter or microscope that was about to be destroyed and give it a name. For example, once I noticed that students were about to push a microscope off a table. I shouted out, "Get your hands off of Fred," and they looked at me as if I were crazy. Then I grabbed Fred the microscope and explained that he had character and usefulness and the rest of us needed him. One fall and he'd be killed. The students shrugged their shoulders and left Fred alone the rest of the year.

The more I taught, the easier it became to anticipate and therefore defuse potential problems. Many of the techniques I learned in the classroom were summarized by a wonderful story I heard Fritz Redl tell about his experience as a disciplinarian. Redl (along with David Wineman) has written the two best books I have seen on discipline, *Children Who Hate* and *Controls from Within* (Free Press). Redl said that once he was director of a summer camp for teenage delinquents. On a hot afternoon, all the youngsters jumped into the lake and swam and played around. After a while one of the boys started getting hostile, dunking other kids who couldn't swim and almost drowning another boy. As Redl put it, there was one first thing he had to do: stop the dunking and get the cause of the problem out of the water. Redl pulled out the offender and sat him down in the sun. Then he had to face what all of us who have to deal with youngsters who make trouble for others face—what comes next? What do you do once the immediate problem has been solved and you have to confront a youngster who expects to be punished or disciplined in some manner. You can't just let go of that moment, because then there's a good chance the problem will develop again. Redl's response to the teenager he pulled out of the water and sat down in the sun (not the shade, he remarked; it would be too comfortable) was: "The reason you're sitting here is that I want you to go swimming. It's hot out here and the water is beautiful and cool. That's where you belong. But you can't go in if you act crazy and make it hard for the other kids to swim and for me. I can't stand watching you. I'd rather be swimming myself, so when you're ready to go in the water and enjoy yourself like the others, go in. And please don't make me pull you out again."

That was it. Redl established the clear boundaries of sensible behavior and put the choice on the boy. He was firm but nonpunitive, clear but nonaccusatory, and most of all positive and sincere about wanting to get the boy back in the water and get things functioning smoothly.

Redl's story represents what I have learned to do with children who for some personal reason act in destructive ways—stop them, make it clear how they have to behave to rejoin the group, and make it clear that the main thing I want to happen is that they rejoin the group. I'm very explicit to even the most severe and bizarre offenders that punishing anyone is a painful, boring experience I try to avoid in any way possible. Yet I make it equally clear that I will stop—forcibly, if necessary—disruptive behavior.

There is another aspect to Redl's example that is essential to the effectiveness of the technique he described. The sun is hot and the water is attractive. In a boring classroom where learning is not much more than filling out forms and taking tests, there's little reason to want to join back in once you've been separated from the group. I've known many children who'd rather sit in the principal's office or on a chair in the hall or in the corner than join the group in performing tedious and oppressive tasks. Decent nonviolent discipline will only be effective in a learning environment where interesting things are happening. There is an essential relationship between the quality of content and the use of nonpunitive discipline strategies in any learning situation. Effective discipline is dependent upon building an attractive and comfortable world that children don't want to be excluded from, and not upon how you respond in any particular instance.

This is as true for the majority of children as for the obviously disruptive few. Boredom is also a discipline problem for conscientious teachers, though one that can easily be ignored. A bored child can seem compliant and even perform very well. But the inner resentment and resistance that accompanies boredom is just as defiant and demoralizing as fighting or cursing. In 1965, I was asked to teach a class in psychology and the working of the mind by a group of teenagers who were the older brothers and sisters of former students of mine. I don't remember what triggered their request, but the first session is still vivid to me. The group of ten gathered in the office of Teachers and Writers Collaborative at Teachers College, Columbia. I had planned to introduce psychology by drawing a number of diagrams of the structure of the mind that would illustrate the differences between Freudian, Adlerian, and Jungian theories of behavior. About halfway through my presentation, I noticed that no one was paying attention. The students acted bored, began to drum on their desks quietly, and acted as if they were in a public school classroom where they could neither leave nor object to what they were being taught. The presence of school habits was keeping us apart. So I deliberately started making spelling errors on the board and statements that were obviously ridiculous and contradictory. For example: Nobody ever has a choice to make; and Every act involves choice. Or: The mind does not exist, only the body; and There is no body, the world is just mind.

After a while, several of the girls timidly raised their hands. Dolores, the girl who got me into teaching the class in the first place, said, "Mr. Kohl, I think you spelled 'motivation' wrong." My response was that I did it deliberately, and also spelled "conscious" *consious*, "dream" *draem*, and "location" *locomotion*. I told Dolores and the rest of the students that since I was as bored as they apparently were, I felt like playing. Then I asked them what they really wanted to learn from the class. I challenged them to clarify their motives and tried to convey the feeling that it was important for me to teach them what they wanted to learn. Teaching was and is my passion, and that idea seemed to have shocked them into realizing that I wasn't interested in grades or obedience but in learning. They let me know that the main thing they wanted to understand was how to make important decisions such as falling in love, choosing work, deciding when to fight and when to walk away. I told them that I didn't have the answers but could expose them to the ideas of people who thought and wrote about the questions. We spent a year pursuing these explorations, and I feel prouder about overcoming this problem of discipline and learning than about any fight I ever broke up or argument I helped solve.

PART 4

CONCLUSION: WHY TEACH?

Recently, a number of college students asked me whether I would have become a teacher during the 1980s, when jobs are tight, public schools are not widely respected, and teaching is treated as a disreputable profession. I was surprised to discover that my answer wasn't a quick "yes." The availability of jobs was one factor that caused me to hesitate. When I graduated from Teachers College, Columbia, in 1962, public school teaching jobs were easy to find. There were no threats of layoffs and the schools were filled with young teachers. Also, the schools were looked at as part of the civil rights struggle and other movements for social and economic democracy. Teaching was part of reforms and innovations larger than the schools and many of us felt proud to be part of them. We had the responsibility of educating children for a decent society. We also felt, perhaps incorrectly, that education and in particular public school education had a central role in the creation of democracy. It was possible to believe that though most public schools were terrible, they could become excellent and serve all children in our society. That belief is no longer widely held. Would I want to become a public school teacher when I am no longer sure that it is possible to transform the public schools into open, exciting centers of learning staffed by people who know how to help all children learn?

Twenty years of wonderful times with children and many defeats in trying to reform schools have made me hesitate about whether I would begin again now.

There are other negative aspects. Pay is low, there are many schools that are practically in states of open warfare between students and teachers, supply budgets are being cut, community support has often turned to community hostility. There are many reasons not to teach, especially in the public schools, and they can't be easily dismissed.

Why teach, then? Are there reasons that override these negatives and can make teaching a wonderful way to spend a life? The answer for some people—and I'm one of them—is, finally, yes, because there still are the children. The prime reason to teach is wanting to be with young people and help them grow. The long-term rewards of seeing your students become decent and creative adults are hard to understand at the beginning of a teaching career. Your major concern is getting through the year. After teaching awhile, however, and remaining in contact with some of your graduates awhile, you understand how important it can be for young people to have a teacher who cares about their growth or introduces them to something that becomes of lifelong value to them. I began teaching when I was twenty-five and my students were twelve. Now I'm forty-five and those youngsters are in their thirties. There's not as much difference between forty-five and thirty-two as between twenty-five and twelve. Your students catch up with you and quite often end up knowing more than you do. It's wonderful to witness that continuous growth at the same time as you're taking on another new group of youngsters.

A number of my own teachers exposed me to aspects of learning and life that I can't imagine being without now. Some also conveyed a sense of my worth and creativity that I've come to internalize and integrate. I grew up in a house with few books and little music. I owe to my high school music teacher my first knowledge of Mozart, and to Mrs. Berstein, my English teacher, the conviction that poetry is important. These might seem like small gifts, but there are people who cannot live without Mozart or poetry, who might never have been writers or mathematicians if some teacher hadn't seen the ability in them and given them the chance to begin cultivating it. The need to stimulate and nurture is especially true now when so many youngsters of every class are exposed to TV, to workbooks, and to structured learning programs that don't touch the mind, much less the heart.

There is a crying need for us to be there for the children. Upon reflection, all of the reasons I've given not to teach are themselves the most compelling reasons to be teaching these days. The time of greatest need for children to be cared for and well educated is during a time of neglect. It is wonderful to be teaching in the midst of a social movement like the civil rights movement, as I did at the beginning of my career. But it is much more important to be teaching now, when society is indifferent and hope for a decent future for all children is considered romantic and even foolish. The loneliness of trying to teach well during cynical times also provides rewards. Young people and their parents know who cares, and there is a warmth and a sense of common struggle that comes from caring when it's easy to be cynical. And the children themselves can come alive and their minds unfold because of one teacher, perhaps in a school at war or in a suburban desert. You can see and feel your students grow, and that finally is the reason to teach and the reward of teaching. Yes, if I were beginning now, I would again put myself through Teachers College to get a credential and find some job teaching in a public school.